MW01093134

The FRENCH & INDIAN WAR

in

WESTERN PENNSYLVANIA

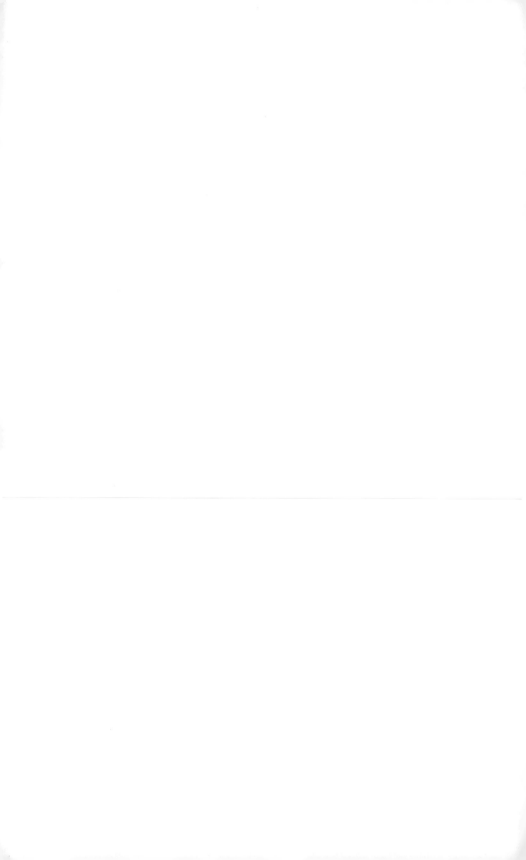

The FRENCH & INDIAN WAR

in

WESTERN PENNSYLVANIA

ROBERT M. DUNKERLY

THE
History
PRESS

Published by The History Press
Charleston, SC
www.historypress.com

Copyright © 2024 by Robert M. Dunkerly
All rights reserved

First published 2024

Manufactured in the United States

ISBN 9781467156172

Library of Congress Control Number: 2023947097

Notice: The information in this book is true and complete to the best of our knowledge. It is offered without guarantee on the part of the author or The History Press. The author and The History Press disclaim all liability in connection with the use of this book.

All rights reserved. No part of this book may be reproduced or transmitted in any form whatsoever without prior written permission from the publisher except in the case of brief quotations embodied in critical articles and reviews.

CONTENTS

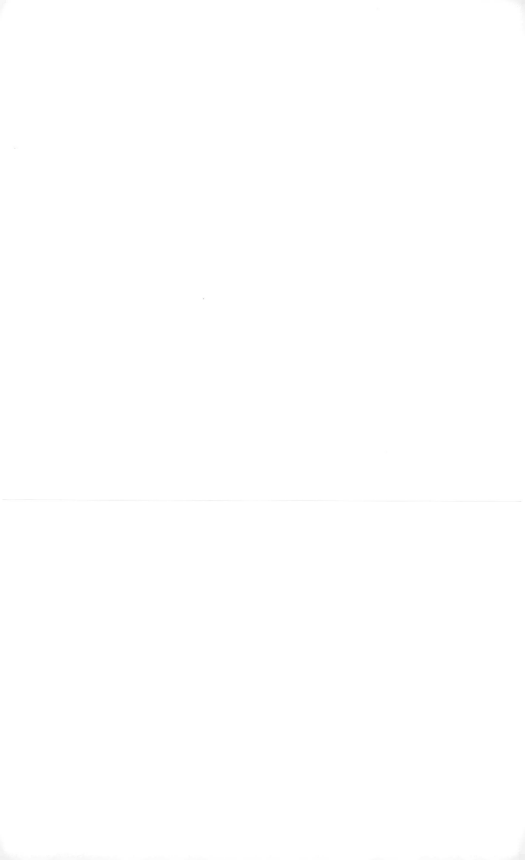

MAPS

BY EDWARD ALEXANDER

PREFACE

It seems I have been following George Washington all my life. Like Washington, my first battlefields were Jumonville Glen and Fort Necessity, though I was a visitor, not a participant. My family also owns land in Somerset County, Pennsylvania, through which a trace of Braddock's Road runs. I've walked it countless times.

The story fascinated me—a tale with so many twists and turns; warfare on the frontier, far from European settlements; and Natives caught up in a struggle to survive. It's a story that links the far-flung cities of Quebec, Paris, London, Williamsburg, Philadelphia, Pittsburgh, Montreal, Logstown and others.

The story is so much more than Washington, but he remains a central figure. I hope to have done justice for the Virginians and Pennsylvanians, Delaware and Shawnee, Scotch Irish and Germans, French and Canadiens and the Mingos and Iroquois.

Written along Braddock's Road
Somerset County, Pennsylvania

There are many terms for the Indigenous people of North America, and preferences for those terms have varied over time and among peoples. Some prefer Native American, *others* Indian. *The History Press uses* Native *as its standard term. Where possible throughout the text, individual nations are named in their own language:* Haudenosaunee *and* Leni Lenape, *for example.*

ACKNOWLEDGEMENTS

My thanks go to the many people who helped with this project: historians with Emerging Revolutionary War, Dan Welch, Phill Greenwalt and Rob Orrison; my good friend and exploring partner Mike Kelly; Brian Reedy and Josh Freeman with Fort Necessity National Battlefield; Patrick Jenks of the Fort LeBoeuf Historical Society; Shawn MacIntyre of the Braddock Battlefield History Center; Mary Manges, the executive director of Fort Ligonier; and Ron Sehn, who helps preserve Fort Dewart. Edward Alexander made the outstanding maps with attention to detail, and Citadel professor Dr. David Preston reviewed several chapters. Neil Bender has been an important local contact, and I appreciate his efforts to preserve local history. Jack Giblin was my supervisor and a great mentor at Bushy Run Battlefield, my very first park. Banks Smither with The History Press has been a great editor, and I appreciate his support for this project, his insights and his advice. My uncle Thomas O'Neil has always shared his passion for western Pennsylvania's history, culture and sports. Sarah Nance has always supported all my efforts and walked a bit on Braddock's Road with me. Sarah and Albert also helped me track down a hard-to-find site in the woods for this book.

1

A COUNTRY BETWEEN

We live in a Country Between, therefore the Land
belongs to neither one nor t'other.
—*Tanacharison, the Seneca Half King, to the French, 1753*

Ascend one of the ridges in central Pennsylvania and look west from the summit. Unfolding before you are undulating parallel ridges running southwest to northeast. The Allegheny Mountains both form a rocky barrier and funnel travel through their fertile valleys.

Settlement of the region dates to nineteen thousand years ago, as proven by the incredible archaeological site at Meadowcroft, Pennsylvania, near the Ohio border. This rock shelter is one of the oldest sites of human habitation in North America.

The Ohio country, the land to the west of those wooded ridges, became home to various Native groups in the 1720s, including the Delaware, Shawnee, Wyandot and Mingo. The Mingos were Seneca and Cayuga from western New York State who had settled in the Ohio Country. Politically, the area was claimed by the Six Nations, or Iroquois, whose homeland was Upstate New York. In their native language, the Iroquois called themselves the Haudenosaunee.[1]

In the 1600s, the Haudenosaunee (consisting of the Oneida, Onondaga, Mohawk, Seneca, Cayuga and, later, the Tuscarora) had conquered the Delaware and managed their political affairs and spoke for them diplomatically. The Six Nations also dictated where they could settle. The

Left: Meadowcroft is one of the most important archaeological sites in North America. The rock shelter near the Ohio-Pennsylvania border has been used for nineteen thousand years. *Author's collection.*

Below: The northeast Natives lived in villages such as this, with long houses surrounded by wooden palisades. *Author's collection.*

Delaware called themselves *Leni Lenape*, which means "real people" or "original people" in their Algonquian language.[2]

Native diplomacy used kinship terms to describe relationships. The Iroquois had political control over the Leni Lenape and referred to them as women, while the Delaware called the Iroquois their uncles. The term *woman* was not intended to be derogatory, as a more accurate translation might be "lady" or "matron." The Iroquoian word they used for the Delaware was *gantowisas*, or "a woman with status and responsibility."[3]

Into this world of Native warfare, diplomacy and settlement came Europeans—the French from Canada and the English from the coast. The Iroquois maintained their control over the Natives of the Ohio Country during King George's War (1744–48) between Britain and France. As tensions with the French grew in the 1750s, the Haudenosaunee insisted that New York, Pennsylvania and other colonies go through them in negotiations with the Natives of the Ohio Country.[4]

Several important Native towns were located throughout the Ohio Country. Many were established in the 1720s, '30s and '40s, as the Delaware, Shawnee and Mingo moved into the region from eastern Pennsylvania. They were centers of trade and diplomacy:

- Queen Aliquippa's Town was founded by this Seneca chief in the 1740s. It was located at modern McKee's Rocks, Pennsylvania. Aliquippa would be an ally of the British in the coming conflict. The elderly woman had met William Penn decades before, when he came to visit his lands, and nearly every emissary into the region met with her, including Washington and Celeron.[5]
- Chartier's Town was founded by Peter Chartier, a French and Shawnee fur trader. The site was along the Allegheny River at the modern site of Tarentum. Mostly Shawnee resided here, and it was a center of trade in the region.[6]
- Kittaning was a Delaware town located along the Allegheny River at the site of the modern town of the same name. It was established in the 1720s and destroyed by Pennsylvania troops in 1756.[7]
- Kuskuski (or Kuskusky) stood near modern New Castle and was settled by the Delaware and Iroquois.[8]
- Logstown, now at Ambridge on the Ohio River, was unusual in that it was a village with a wall of upright logs. It was an

important diplomatic and trading center and home to Iroquois, Delaware, Wyandots, Shawnee and Mohicans. It was known as Shenango among the Natives and Chinique to the French.[9]
- Murdering Town (or Murthering Town) stood on Connoquenessing Creek, near modern Evans City, Pennsylvania. Washington was nearly killed near this Delaware village, which existed before the incident. The origin of the name is obscure; the Leni Lenape called it Sancock.
- Shannopin's Town stood on the east bank of the Allegheny River, about two miles from the Forks of the Ohio River (The Point). Seneca founded the village in the 1730s.[10]
- Venango was located at the mouth of French Creek in modern Franklin. English traders set up a trading post here prior to the outbreak of the war.

Although divided by language and nationality, the woodland Natives of the Ohio Country shared a similar culture and lifestyle. They followed a seasonal rhythm of life with roots that stretched back centuries, with knowledge and skills from ancestors passed down through the generations. Yet no knowledge or skill in their collective memory could prepare them for the violent and radical changes to come in the last decades of the eighteenth century.

The various groups in the Ohio Country used their own terms to describe its landscape and name its places. The French called the Monongahela River the Theaudaogpin. In Algonquian, *monongahela* means "falling banks," a description of the river's crumbling shoreline.[11]

The French and Indian War has often been seen in terms of European-Native diplomacy and military thrusts launched by the Europeans. Natives are generally seen only in supportive roles, providing assistance in exchange for trade goods and forming military alliances. Beneath the neat and smooth surface of European negotiation and formal military campaigns lies a complex and interconnected web of Native diplomacy and military agendas. The Natives are central to this story, and they acted with the history of long, complicated intertribal relationships fresh in their minds, a point that most Europeans never fully understood.

It was the Natives who held the key to success in the war in western Pennsylvania, and their involvement in the French and Indian War was largely a continuation of existing tribal rivalries and policies. Nor were divisions on the European side simply clear cut between the English and

Left: One of the most important Native settlements in the region was Logstown, located along the Ohio River west of modern Pittsburgh. Today, a cluster of markers notes the site. *Author's collection.*

Below: Trade was one of the things that brought settlers into the Ohio Country and which motivated the Native tribes to form alliances with Europeans. Common trade goods included copper jewelry and glass beads. *Author's collection.*

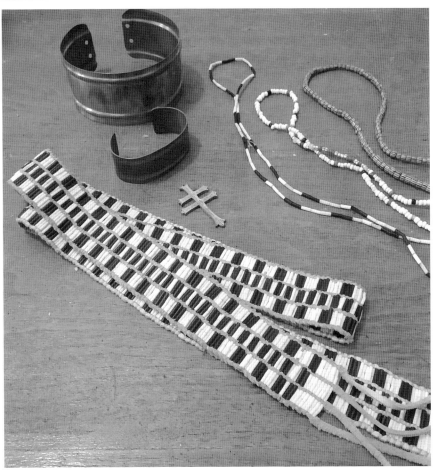

French, as various intercolonial rivalries clouded the picture. English colonial divisions undercut the efforts of British troops to act efficiently, as did antagonism between Canadien milice (militia) and French regular troops on the other side. Thus, the negotiations between Europeans and Natives became ensnared in internal political rivalries on both sides.

The movements of the British and French armies have overshadowed the importance of Native negotiation during the War for Empire in Pennsylvania. It is important to bear in mind that Native groups were highly mobile, and throughout the colonial period, they shifted their homes and their alliances. During the early eighteenth century, the Delaware (Leni Lenape) were gradually pushed out of their homes in modern Delaware, New Jersey and the southeastern corner of Pennsylvania. Settling along the Susquehanna, by the 1730s, they were temporarily beyond the reach of English encroachment. Soon, some Delaware were moving farther west, and the eastern and western bands became two distinct groups. They were culturally similar but geographically separate.[12]

The appearance of European troops during the coming war offered the Natives of the Ohio Country new opportunities to seek independence. By the mid-1750s, the Anglo-French rivalry that divided North America and that was the cause of previous wars began to heat up again—this time in the Ohio Country. At the time, English colonization hugged the Atlantic seaboard, while the French settlements were concentrated in New Orleans and along the St. Lawrence River. To cut the English off from the interior of North America, France built outposts along the Mississippi River and the Great Lakes, but they were widely scattered. In 1753, the French launched an invasion of the Ohio Country to strengthen their claim on the area and take the strategic junction of the Ohio, Allegheny, and Monongahela Rivers at present-day Pittsburgh.[13]

Not only did England and France claim the Ohio Valley, but the Iroquois claimed it as well. The Six Nations followed a careful policy of neutrality, playing the English and French against each other. They had been following this successful strategy since the first European incursions of the seventeenth century and continued it through the Revolution and the War of 1812. The English had made treaties of friendship with the Six Nations and felt that they would oppose the French incursion. The Iroquois did but on the grounds that it was theft of their land, a point lost on English policy makers. The western tribes of the Haudenosaunee, the Cayuga and the Seneca generally leaned toward the French, while the eastern tribes of the Onondaga, the Oneida and the Mohawk were more pro-English. A delicate alliance held the Iroquois together. William Johnson, an English Indian agent and representative of the Crown, would be a key player in negotiating with the Iroquois. The growing conflict threatened the stability of the confederacy as never before.[14]

The western Delaware and Shawnee of the Ohio Country, eager to throw off Iroquois rule, reluctantly embraced the French and their cherished trade goods. Friendship with the French was a double-edged sword; it provided access to spirits, blankets, tools, weapons and ammunition, but it tied them to one European nation. The eastern Leni Lenape largely remained neutral, hoping to win the favor of Pennsylvania Quakers. To make the mix more complex, the Ohio and Allegheny Valleys were claimed by three English colonies: Virginia, Pennsylvania and Connecticut. Their rivalries would hurt English war efforts, and complicate English-Native negotiations tremendously.[15]

The Iroquois of Upstate New York projected their power into the Ohio Country through rulers they placed over the Natives living there. Tanacharison was a fifty-three-year-old Seneca in 1753 and was known as the Half King. He represented Haudenosaunee authority in the Ohio Country but was not himself an independent ruler. Scaroudy, also called Montacatootha, was an Oneida Half King in the region who directed the Shawnee.[16]

Tensions rose among the Natives through the 1730s and 1740s. The colony of Pennsylvania appointed farmer, minister and land speculator Conrad Weiser as its interpreter and diplomat to negotiate with the Iroquois. Weiser negotiated several treaties and land purchases in the 1740s and 1750s. As a youth, he had lived with the Mohawk and understood and respected their culture.[17]

Pennsylvania's southern and western boundaries were disputed at this time, and the Ohio Valley was claimed by Virginia based on the colony's seventeenth-century charter. In October 1753, Governor Robert Dinwiddie of Virginia sent twenty-one-year-old militia colonel George Washington as a messenger to warn the French troops on the Allegheny River that they were on English land (specifically Virginia land) and request that they leave. Not surprisingly, they refused, claiming that the land belonged to the French by earlier exploration. The following year, the bloodshed began.[18]

Pennsylvania had no colonial militia due to the opposition of its Quaker-dominated assembly. In fact, there was a great deal of political fighting between the assembly and the Penn family, who owned the colony. The colony also had challenges with its northern boundary (disputed with Connecticut) and its southern boundary (disputed with Maryland).

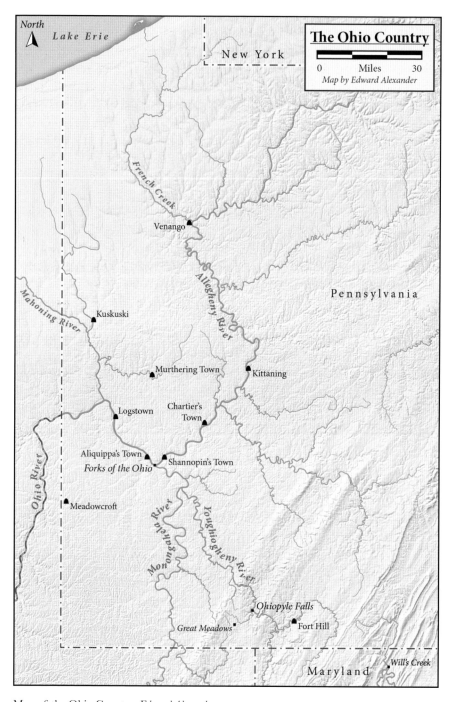

Map of the Ohio Country. *Edward Alexander.*

With the area firmly in French hands, an influx of pro-French western tribes, such as the Ottawas, Hurons, Pottawatomies, Wyandots and Chippewa, joined the war. Known as the *Pays den Haut* (French meaning "from the upper country," west of Montreal), these Natives from the Great Lakes area were firm allies of the French and were traditional enemies of the Iroquois. Many of the Ohio Valley's Delaware and Shawnee awaited further developments before choosing a side in the quickly escalating conflict; yet they were leaning strongly toward the French. The English appeared to be losing; the Pays den Haut had moved in, and an alliance with the French offered the prospect of autonomy from the Haudenosaunee.[19]

Throughout the French and Indian War and its violent offshoot, Pontiac's War, various intertribal rivalries flared up. The Delaware and Shawnee of the Ohio Valley struck out against the Iroquois, who, in turn, attempted to reassert their authority. Eastern and western bands of the Leni Lenape faced different challenges during the struggle. The conflict also drew in Great Lakes tribes, such as the Ottawa, the Ojibwa, the Huron and the Pottawattamie, who raided their eastern enemies. In the process of acting in their tribal self-interests, the Natives sided with various European powers. The English were divided by rivalries between Maryland, Virginia, Connecticut and Pennsylvania, as well as discord between colonial assemblies and governors. While on the surface, the war's flow appeared smooth, a complex round of diplomatic maneuvering took place on both the frontier and in the capital cities of Europe. No British or French military victory came without careful Native negotiation.

The region entered a brief period of relative peace, yet violence soon erupted again after 1765. Settlers poured into the region, enflaming hostilities with the Natives. Pennsylvania and Virginia launched an undeclared war, with rival militias invading the region. The boundary disputes of these Mid-Atlantic states would not be firmly resolved for several more decades.

In 1774, Virginia's governor Lord Dunmore launched a raid into the territory to defeat the Shawnee and secure the land. The Pennsylvania and Virginia militias competed for control of the region. The outbreak of the Revolution again allowed the Native groups to choose sides and consolidate their positions. In another grueling round of frontier warfare that lasted until 1783, western Pennsylvania's Native population was largely dispersed by violence, disease and migration.

From the 1750s through 1783, violence in western Pennsylvania pitted Europeans against Natives for thirty years. Yet it was much more complicated than that, as the Delaware and the Shawnee subverted the efforts of Iroquois,

Chestnut Ridge was one of the many mountain ranges that runs through southwestern Pennsylvania. *Author's collection.*

and troops from Pennsylvania, Virginia and Connecticut sparred among themselves while fighting for England against France. Since few contemporary European or colonial observers fully understood the complexity of the negotiations and maneuvers between these various factions, the story that has come down to us often dilutes and simplifies the reality.

It is ironic and unfortunate that Pennsylvania's Native population was decimated by war and forced migration, events that occurred in a colony dedicated to peaceful relations. Sadder still is the fact that there are few tangible reminders of the Native population that remain other than place names. There are no reservations or tribal lands in the state today.

The people of the Ohio Country longed to control their new settlements free of outside interference. Their ancestors had been driven from their traditional homes across the mountains, where the *kizis* (sun) rises. Over time, the Natives grew dependent on European trade goods for survival, adapting European-made cloth for clothing and using metal pots and kettles for cooking and powder and shot for hunting. As this happened, the knowledge and use of bows and arrows died off by the 1750s.

From the mid-eighteenth century to the early nineteenth century, the Natives of the Ohio Country and the Great Lakes region experienced a cycle of wars. While historians divide them up neatly into compartments like the French and Indian War, Pontiac's War, Dunmore's War, the Revolution and the War of 1812, there never really was a period of peace, just breaks between the violence.

Sites to Explore

Conrad Weiser Homestead
28 Weiser Lane | Womelsdorf, PA 19567
610-589-2934 | www.conradweiserhomestead.org
GPS: 40 36.0641, -76 17.4169

The home of the prominent Native negotiator, this historic site includes his home and grave. Its special events throughout the year focus on Weiser's life and the period of the French and Indian War.

Logstown Historic Markers

From 1727 to 1758, this was one of the largest Native towns in the region. Several important conferences took place here before and during the French and Indian War. Washington visited in the winter of 1753 on his mission to confront the French. There are two sites that commemorate the village.

Several historic markers stand at the intersection of Duss Avenue and Anthony Wayne Drive in Baden, Pennsylvania, 15005. GPS: 40 37.372, -80 13.592.

Another cluster of markers stands about one thousand feet away at the intersection of Logan Lane and Route 65. GPS: 40 62.7907, -80 24.1832. There are no facilities at either site.

Meadowcroft Rockshelter and Historic Village
401 Meadowcroft Road | Avella, PA 15312
www.heinzhistorycenter.org/meadowcroft
GPS: 40 17.176, -80 29.521

The centerpiece of this historic site is the rock shelter, which dates human habitation to nineteen thousand years ago. It was also the site of a sixteenth-century Native village, a 1770s frontier trading post and a nineteenth-century village.

STATE MUSEUM OF PENNSYLVANIA
300 NORTH STREET | HARRISBURG, PA 17120
717-787-4980 | WWW.STATEMUSEUMPA.ORG
GPS: 40 26.5708, -76 88.5757

This is the state's museum of history and natural history. It has exhibits featuring Natives and archaeology.

Other sites of importance, identified later in this book, include the Fort Pitt Museum and the Heinz History Center in Pittsburgh.

2

FRENCH INVASION

To take possession of the Ohio.
—French officers at Fort LeBoeuf

The strangers arrived by *nibi* (Algonquian for "water"), coming down the big lake. There were many of them, and they clearly intended to stay, unlike the few white traders who had previously penetrated the Natives' territory. They were French troops coming to claim and possess the Ohio Country.

The French first settled what is now Canada in 1608 in Quebec, and the fledging town became the colony's capital. The name Canada is derived from the Iroquoian word *kanata*, meaning "village." The first French settlement at Quebec derives its name from the Algonquian word meaning "strait" or "narrows," referring to the narrowing of the St. Lawrence River at that place. The French settlers came to call themselves Canadiens.

By the middle of the 1700s, France's claim to the vast interior of North America was anchored on its settlements in Montreal, Quebec and New Orleans. There were few permanent French settlements in between, and the closest to the Ohio Country were Forts Niagara and Detroit. It was a big void.

The British colonies, by contrast, were growing rapidly and solidly from Massachusetts to Georgia. As the British and Americans pushed west, they started on a collision course with the French. In 1748, wealthy Virginia investors formed the Ohio Company to claim and sell land on the Virginia

Quebec was the capital of New France and was a strategically important city. Trade goods and supplies arrived here from France to sustain the war effort. *New York Public Library.*

frontier. Its members included Lieutenant Governor Robert Dinwiddie and Lawrence Augustine Washington, whose half brother George was a land surveyor.[1]

Pennsylvania also claimed land west of the mountains, though its efforts to physically occupy this land were weaker. Few Pennsylvania settlers had ventured west beyond the Cumberland Valley, as the Allegheny Mountains stood like a barrier to settlement. The bulk of the colony's population lived in its southeast corner within one hundred miles of Philadelphia.

The French needed to exert power and put teeth into their claim on the Ohio Country, so in 1749, Pierre Joseph Celeron de Blainville attempted to do just that. He left Montreal with 213 men, traveling by water to the Ohio Country. His second-in-command was Claude Pierre Pècaudy de Contrecoeur. Another officer in the expedition was Coulon de Villiers. Both would return and play important roles in the Ohio Country. The expedition floated down the Allegheny River to the Ohio River (the French considered them one river, la Belle Riviere). They buried seven lead plates at key points, physically claiming the land.[2]

On July 29, the expedition fastened the French coat of arms to a tree and buried a plate at the mouth of Conewango Creek on the Allegheny River, now modern Warren, Pennsylvania. The plates were about eleven inches long, seven and a half inches wide and one-eighth of an inch thick. A blank space was left for the date and location to be added at the deposit site.[3]

The plates were meant to tangibly reaffirm France's claim, stating their purpose "of the renewal of possession which we have taken of the said river Ohio, and all of those which fall into it, and of all the territories on both sides as far as the source of said rivers." The expedition spent three days at Logstown, which the French called Chinique. On August 3, 1749, de Celoron wrote in his diary, "Buried a lead plate on the south bank of the Ohio river, four leagues below the Riviere Aux Boeufs [modern French Creek], opposite a bald mountain and near a large stone on which are many figures crudely engraved."[4]

Along the way, they warned any English traders they encountered to leave and informed the Natives they met that the French were claiming the land. They continued down la Belle Riviere, eventually going as far as Fort Detroit, covering over three thousand miles.[5]

In 1752 a new governor, Ange de Menneville Marquis Duquesne, arrived in Quebec. He was determined to extend French power and influence into the interior of the continent. Writing about his effort in the Ohio Country,

This reproduction Celeron plate is in the Fort Le Bouef Museum. The French buried these plates at intervals along the Allegheny and Ohio Rivers and others to physically claim their territory. *Author's collection.*

Duquesne stated that he would send a force "to go and seize and establish itself on the Belle Riviere, which we are on the verge of losing if I do not make this hasty but indisputable effort."[6]

Garrisoning the forts and towns of New France were the Les Compagnies Frances del a Marine (Independent Companies of Marines). These were individual companies, not a single regiment, and they were deployed to New France to serve on ships or garrison fortifications. The men were French, and officers tended to be Canadien-born. Working with the Canadien milice (militia), they were the military force at Duquesne's disposal as conflict heated up with the English.

From Quebec City, the French projected power across a vast part of the continent: down the Ohio and Mississippi Rivers to the Gulf of Mexico and west to the Great Lakes. Their claim clashed with several English colonies, notably Virginia. From Williamsburg, Virginia laid claimed the land from its southern border directly west and northwest from the Potomac River to include the Great Lakes, resulting in ongoing issues with Maryland and Pennsylvania. And in their capital town of Onondaga in Upstate New York, the Iroquois projected power south through the Ohio Country and down to the Carolinas. Despite the intentions of the French and the maps they drew to support their claims, reality was often different on the ground. Claims on paper and even forts built to physically occupy territory did not convey actual control.

This was not the first time the French clashed with the British over territory in North America—far from it—but this time, the stakes were higher. The European settlements were on a collision course, having consumed more land and grown in the years since the end of King George's War, the previous conflict, in 1748. The coming struggle was for keeps.

What is commonly called the French and Indian War was the fourth such conflict between France and England in North America, and it was one that became global in scale. From 1688 to 1697, the two countries fought King William's War. Then from 1702 to 1713, they fought Queen Anne's War. Next, from 1744 to 1748, they fought King George's War. Peace was always tentative—really just a break to prepare for the next conflict. For half of this sixty-year period, the two nations were at war. In 1753, just four years after de Blainville's plate-depositing voyage and one year after Governor Duquesne's arrival, the French sent an armed expedition to occupy the Ohio Country.

Captain Paul Marin de la Malgue, seur de Marin, was a Montreal-born officer who had been in the military for over thirty years. He led

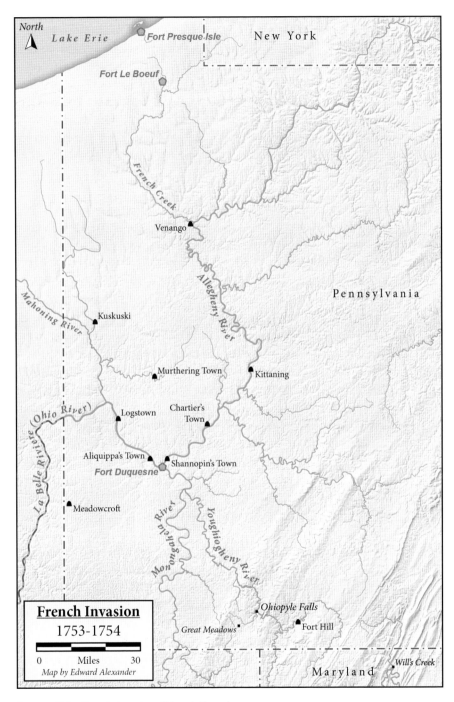

A map of the French invasion. *Edward Alexander.*

the expeditionary force that included 300 troupes des marines and about 1,700 Canadien milice. That summer, Half King Tanacharison (a Seneca representing the Iroquois authority in the region) met with Marin to protest the French arrival, but Marin insisted they were here to stay and refused the half king's wampum, a diplomatic refusal of the highest order. The Half King's Haudenosaunee were too few to make an impression on the French, and the Europeans were too ill-supplied and weak to be threating to the Natives; thus, both groups were dissatisfied but not strong enough to force the issue. There, the stalemate rested.[7]

As the French worked diligently to build their string of forts in the summer of 1753, their effort was plagued by several problems. Water was low in French Creek (which the French called Riviere aux Boeufs), making passage difficult. Supplies ran low, the work was exhausting and illness broke out among the troops.[8]

Governor Duquesne said of the milice, "The Canadians are the only people in the world who would be capable of sleeping in the open air, and able to endure the immense labor which this detachment performed in transporting baggage on two portages, one of seven thousand leagues and the other of three leagues." (A league is equivalent to about three miles.)[9]

Construction began on the first fort, Fort Presque Isle, overlooking Lake Erie, on May 3, and by August 3, it was substantially finished. Its walls were twelve to fifteen feet high and were made using horizontal logs with a six-foot-wide section filled with earth. It would have been a formidable structure. The logs used in its construction came from native chestnut trees.[10]

The fort sat on a small hill west of the mouth of Mill Creek, overlooking the entrance to the bay. One Native account, relayed by Scaroudy, noted, "The fort on the big lake is very strong with hewed timbers about six feet apart filled with dirt, with four bastions and a ditch."[11]

A French soldier described arriving there in 1754: "April 24th, we arrived almost at the foot of Lake Erie, at a place called Presque Isle. It is a rather shallow bay into which we entered, and where the ground plan of a fort was being laid out, after an abattis of trees had been made. The fort was built of squared timbers with four bastions mounting twelve cannon which we had brought." Another soldier, Jolicoeur Charles Bonin, described the plentiful game around the post. Bonin wrote of hunting elk, deer, bear, swans, geese, turkey, partridges, ducks and pigeons nearby.[12]

Following the French and Indian War, the British built a fort on the site in 1760, but it was attacked and burned by Natives in Pontiac's War. The young American nation built a third fort nearby, east of Mill Creek, in 1795.

The Fort Presque Isle site. A series of historic markers note it was the site of the French fort that looked out over the bay. From here, the French invasion moved south, toward La Belle Riviera. *Author's collection.*

The site of the French fort was destroyed by the construction of a brickyard in the 1800s.[13]

From Fort Presque Isle, the French troops began constructing a portage road to the south. By June, the French had advanced seventeen miles to begin work on the next post in their chain of fortifications, Fort Le Boeuf. Construction here began on July 12. Washington described it as being built of "upright piles" during his visit a year later.[14]

The fort's four bastions had eight six-pound cannons and one four-pound gun at the gate, considerable firepower for this remote part of the world. Inside the fort was a guardhouse, a chapel, the physician's lodgings and the commander's private stores. Outside were several log barracks, some covered with bark and others with boards.[15]

Sent to assist with transportation—but becoming a burden in and of themselves—were about forty-five horses. The animals required more fodder than could be obtained and soon suffered along with the men.[16]

Farther south at the Native town of Venango, the French evicted English settler John Frazier from his trading post and assumed control of the cabins, storehouse and blacksmith shop he had built there. In the spring of 1754,

Above: The history of the Native tribes in the area is explained on this plaque at the site of Fort Presque Isle. *Author's collection.*

Opposite: The site of Fort Machault is now in a neighborhood overlooking the Allegheny River in Franklin, Pennsylvania. From here, French forces descended to the forks of the Ohio River in 1754. *Author's collection.*

they began the construction of Fort Machault, using Frazier's buildings for shelter in the meantime. Captain Phillipe Thomas de Joncaire assumed control here.[17]

French troops did not complete Fort Machault until 1757. It was named in honor of Jean-Baptiste Machault d'Arnouville, minister of the marine. The fort sat on a rise sixty yards west of the Allegheny River with a bastion of logs eight inches thick and thirteen feet high laid lengthwise. Inside were six ranges of barracks two stories high with stone chimneys; outside, there were more barracks.[18]

The stress of the campaign and its slow pace wore on Marin, and Governor Duquesne, concerned for his health, recalled him. On September 29, sixty-one-year-old Captain Legardeur de Sainte Pierre was dispatched

to take over the forces operating on la Belle Riviere from the ailing Marin. St. Pierre arrived after Marin died. The campaign had taken its toll on the troops as well, with only about eight hundred of the original two thousand still fit for duty by fall.[19]

One French officer wrote of the work:

> *The labor of our troops was excessive. The soldiers, sunk half-leg deep in mud, and weakened by the recent fatigues of the first portage, succumbed under their burdens. It was impossible to use the few horses that remained. It was an afflicting spectacle to behold these debilitated men, struggling at the same time against the bad season and the difficulties of the road, broken down by the weight of their weapons and of the loads which they had to carry.[20]*

The Iroquois became increasingly concerned with the French incursion and expressed their displeasure at a conference at Fort Presque Isle in early September. On September 3, Half King Tanacharison said, "Evil tidings are innumerable in the lands where we live." He added, "We beg you to tell us in whose name you are coming to set up these establishments." He then directly asked the French not to build forts here and offered a wampum belt, a customary practice in Native negotiations. Lastly, he said to the French, "I will strike over all this Land with my Rod, let it hurt who it will."[21]

Marin refused to accept the wampum, which, to the Iroquois, meant he refused to hear the speech (whether he understood the significance of his actions is not known). He then affirmed that the land belonged to the king of France. Adding insult to injury, he also insisted that Tanachrison spoke for himself, not the Natives of the region.[22]

The French hardly knew the limits of the vast territory they claimed. On July 10, 1753, Governor Duquesne wrote to Marin:

> As I have found nothing in the Secretariat which could inform me about the limits of the Belle Riviere, and as there are commissioners from each side working on them, get information from the Sieur de Joncaire as to where he thinks the borders are; and for the time being you should drive off and pillage all the English who are on our land, and if any would be found on the edge, you will have them informed that if they come to trade among us, they will be arrested and their gods will be pillaged. I remember that I have been told there was a chain of mountains in a southern direction from the Belle Riviere which has always been regarded as the limits of our territory.[23]

Marin passed away in late October at Fort Le Boeuf, and Sainte Pierre now commanded the string of French posts. The French planned to descend la Belle Riviere in the spring of 1754, take the Forks of the Ohio River (where Pittsburgh now stands) and move on to occupy Logstown. So far, nothing had stopped them.[24]

SITES TO EXPLORE

FORT PITT BLOCKHOUSE
601 COMMONWEALTH PLACE, BUILDING C | PITTSBURGH, PA 15222
WWW.FORTPITTBLOCKHOUSE.COM
GPS: 40 26.468, -80 5.81

This is the only original remnant of the fortifications that stood at the Point (Forks of the Ohio) and the oldest building in western Pennsylvania (built in 1764). It is operated as a museum by the Daughters of the American Revolution.

Fort Pitt Museum
Point State Park
601 Commonwealth Place | Pittsburgh, PA 15222
www.heinzhistorycenter.org/fort-pitt
GPS: 40 26.46, -80 5.69

This museum tells the story of military history at the Point in the middle of downtown Pittsburgh. Nearby is the Fort Pitt Blockhouse (see previous entry). Walk the grounds to see an outline of Fort Duquesne and take in the great views at the confluence of the Allegheny, Monongahela and Ohio Rivers—the key to the continent.

Fort Le Boeuf Museum
103 South High Street | Waterford, PA 16441
www.fortleboeufhistory.com/campus/museum
GPS: 41 56.405, -79 58.952

Built near the site of the French fort, the museum has exhibits about the Natives from the area, the fort and the archaeologists who discovered it. French Creek flows by the site; this is where Washington observed bateaux ready for the spring invasion. Across from the museum is a small park with a statue of Washington and several markers, and to the north of it is the 1810 Judson House, a historic home that is open for tours and sits on the site of the fort. The Eagle Hotel rose on the site of the west bastion in 1826.

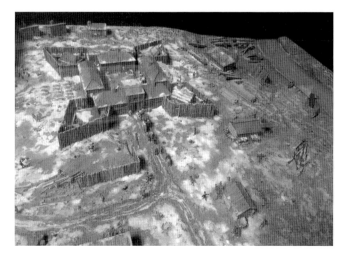

A model in the Fort Le Bouef Museum shows how the fort would have looked in 1753. *Author's collection.*

Fort Machault/Fort Venango Markers
GPS: 41 23.359, -79 49.33

The Native town of Venango is where John Frazier built a trading post that was seized by the French in 1753. Washington stopped here on his way to Fort Le Boeuf. Later, the French built Fort Machault on the site, and after the war, the British occupied it and built Fort Venango.

The sites of these forts are gone, and there is no historic site or museum there today. Two historic markers stand at the intersection of Eighth Street (U.S. 322) and Elk Street in Franklin, Pennsylvania. Just down Elk Street, within sight of the others, is a stone marker for the fort site.

There are no facilities at this site.

The site of Fort Machault (later Venango) is marked by this stone monument. Washington stopped by the site before the French fort was built at the Native town of Venango. *Author's collection.*

Fort Presque Isle Site
Parade and East Front Streets
Erie, PA
GPS: 42 13.7568, -80 07.9979

A series of historic markers at the northern end of Parade Street in Erie mark the site of the French fort and discuss the later forts built by British and American forces. Nearby, on the grounds of the Pennsylvania Soldiers Home, is the grave of Revolutionary War general Anthony Wayne.

There are no facilities at this site.

3

THE MESSENGER

Caunotaucarius: *Algonquin for "Town Taker"*

Born in 1732 at Pope's Creek Plantation in Westmoreland County, Virginia, to a moderately wealthy family, George Washington aspired to forge a military career. The Virginia of Washington's youth was rural and sparsely populated; the colony contained less than one hundred thousand souls, settlement reached no farther west than present-day Interstate 95 and the only existing towns of any size were Norfolk and Williamsburg. Washington received only rudimentary schooling; the early death of his father prevented him from having a formal English education.

Washington was the oldest of six, but several of his half siblings were older and likely motivated him to be ambitious rather than rely on inheritance to advance himself. He spent most of his youth in Fredericksburg. He admired his older half brother Lawrence, who owned a plantation called Mount Vernon. As a teenager, George learned surveying and aggressively applied his skill in northern Virginia and on the frontier in the Shenandoah Valley. By the time he reached his twenties, England and France were on a collision course over territory lying between the British coastal settlements and French Canada.

In 1747, several wealthy Virginians formed the Ohio Company, a corporation used to purchase and resell about half a million acres in what is now western Pennsylvania and Ohio. The investors hoped to gain land for themselves, as well as immense profits.[1]

In 1752, Lawrence died of illness, and George inherited Mount Vernon. He also took Lawrence's place as adjutant of the Virginia Militia. Washington was eager to advance his military career and make political connections that would be favorable to someone of his status from a leading Virginia family. Governor Dinwiddie turned to him to take a message to the French in the Ohio Country, warning them to leave English lands. He readily volunteered for the mission and left Williamsburg on October 3, 1753.[2]

At Fredericksburg, Washington hired his old fencing master, a Dutch man named Jacob Van Braam, to accompany him as a translator. Washington spoke no French, and Van Bramm knew some—though perhaps not as much as Washington expected. They would be entering a region few English had explored. One Englishman who knew the Ohio Country well was Christopher Gist, a forty-eight-year-old frontiersman who had been contracted by the Ohio Company to explore its western lands.[3]

Between 1750 and 1751 Gist traveled as far as modern Ohio and Kentucky. Upon returning, Gist oversaw the construction of a storehouse for the Ohio Company at Will's Creek, now Cumberland, Maryland. The location was named for a friendly local Native named Will. The storehouse held trade goods and served as a jumping-off point for exploring and for the intended settlement, using Nemacolin's Path, which ran to the west. Later, Fort Cumberland would rise at the site.[4]

While traveling the Kanawha River toward its junction with the Ohio River, Gist stopped to chisel on a big rock along the bank this inscription:

THE OHIO COMPANY
FEBy 1751
BY CHRISTOPHER GIST

Gist claimed some land himself and settled his family on a plantation north of modern Uniontown, Pennsylvania. Washington met Gist at Will's Creek and requested that he accompany them. His knowledge of the Natives and the territory and his survival skills were all invaluable. The party now included Washington, Gist, Van Braam and four servants, and they all traveled on horseback.[5]

They took Nemacolin's Path west from the Will's Creek storehouse. Nemacolin, a Delaware, had blazed the path over the high ridges of modern-day western Maryland with Gist. Crossing the mountains, they experienced "excessive Rains and vast Quantity of Snow." On November

ROBERT DINWIDDIE.
Governor of Virginia.

Left: Robert Dinwiddie was the governor of Virginia, as well as an investor in the Ohio Company. Today, a county south of Petersburg is named in his honor. *New York Public Library*.

Right: A sketch of young Colonel Washington. *New York Public Library*.

22, the party reached John Frazier's cabin at the mouth of Turtle Creek on the Monongahela River. Frazier was the trader who had been forced out of Venango earlier that year by the French.[6]

The next day they reached the Forks of the Ohio River at the Point. Washington observed, "The Rivers are each a Quarter of a Mile, or more, across." Washington's military eye scanned the area with a view toward occupying and defending the location. He noted, "I spent some Time in viewing the Rivers, and the Land in the Fork, which I think extremely well situated for a Fort, as it had the absolute Command of both Rivers."[7]

Then they journeyed west to the Native town of Logstown on the north bank of the Ohio River (the site is now west of Pittsburgh). From November 24 to November 30, the party lodged here. It was a center of power in the region, and Washington intended to meet with tribal leaders there to gain support for the mission.[8]

When the Natives saw the young stranger and his group arrive, Washington likely seemed impatient, still learning the ways of diplomacy on the frontier. This was Native land, and negotiations would be done on their terms. Half King Tanichrisson knew the matter was important, but he would act on it at his own pace—and with Iroquois interests in mind. Washington could not get the Natives to fully support him; the Ohio tribes were not so sure about siding with the British yet.[9]

Before anything else, Tanichrisson had to return to the French the wampum belts they had been given. It was the proper way to reject the French overtures. Messengers were sent to retrieve them, and in the meantime, the Virginians waited.[10]

The Natives faced difficult decisions. Upriver at the Lenape village of Kittanning on the Allegheny River was another important chief, Shingas, who was assertive against Iroquois rule. Although he was fiercely independent, he leaned toward the British but would soon have to tolerate French rule.

Logstown had fifty cabins, which were inhabited by the Mohawk, Seneca, Oneida and Delaware. It was the site of the 1752 signing of the treaty of friendship between the Ohio Company and the Natives.

Here, Washington met important leaders, such as Half King Tanacharison. Tanacharison was a Seneca and the representative of the Iroquois in the Ohio Country. The English called him the Half King because he did not rule with absolute power but with the control of the Haudenosaunee in New York.

Meeting with the Half King and other leaders, like Scaroudy, Washington gained their approval. The Natives were willing to stand up to the French, who declared that they intended to descend the Allegheny River soon and fortify the Point—and they would brush aside the Natives to do it.[11]

Washington heard the speech the Half King had given to the French earlier, noting his reaction as the French had downplayed and belittled him. The next day, Washington addressed the Natives as "brothers," a more equal family term than *children*.[12]

On November 26, Washington affirmed that the Natives were allies of Virginia, giving a belt of wampum. He did not say why they were going to visit the French. When the Natives asked about the nature of the message he was to deliver, Washington simply noted in his journal that he had anticipated this question and that his answer had satisfied them. What did he actually say? Certainly, he did not say that the Virginians had claimed the land they were all standing on. He simply glossed over that detail.[13]

The days at Logstown were long ones full of waiting, and we can imagine the pacing, tension and wandering of the mind of Major Washington. Finally, the group of eight (Gist, Washington, their interpreter Van Braam, their trader John Davison and four Natives, including three old chiefs and one young hunter) departed for Venango, eighty miles away. Among the Natives was Guyasuta, a Seneca in his late twenties who was a rising spokesman and

At Logstown, Washington met with Native leaders and began his introduction to frontier diplomacy. Here, General Anthony Wayne's forces camped in 1792 on their way to fight on the frontier in modern Ohio. *Author's collection.*

leader among his people. Guyasuta called Washington "Tall Hunter," and the Virginian referred to him as "the Hunter." It was now December, and the journey east crossed frozen fields, swamps and creeks.[14]

The group arrived at the old trading post site at Venango on December 4. The French had occupied the buildings but not yet built their fort (which would be called Fort Machault). Washington described the site as an old Native town on the mouth French Creek. Flying above the house formerly occupied by John Frazier was a French flag. Here, Washington met Captain Phillipe Thomas Joncaire, who was half-Seneca and half-French. Joncaire informed him that he needed to travel up to the next French post at Fort Le Bouef to see the overall commander, St. Pierre.[15]

Washington and his party spent the night, intending to leave the next morning. The Virginian wrote, "The Wine, as they doused themselves pretty plentifully with it, soon banished the Restraint which at fist appear'd in their Conversation, and gave a License to their Tongues to reveal their Sentiments most freely." He continued, "They told me, That it was their absolute Design to take Possession of the Ohio, and by G—they would do it."[16]

The Half King also got drunk and, despite his earlier promise, did not stand up to the French. In fact, Joncaire tried to induce the Natives to stay, separating them from the Virginians. Imagine Washington's state of mind—likely exacerbated after coming all this way and negotiating with the Indians—now seeing it fall apart before his eyes.[17]

The entire group did go on, traveling north through the cold rain over creeks that were running high. On December 11, they arrived at Fort Le Boeuf, hopeful this was their last stop. The next day, Washington arose, expecting to complete his journey, explain his mission and the English position and receive the French reply. It was not to be that easy. The fort's commander, Saint Pierre, a fifty-two-year-old officer with considerable experience, spoke no English. Through translators, he informed Washington that there would be yet another delay. The commander at Fort Presque Isle, Pierre-Jean-Baptiste-Francois-Xavier Legardeur de Repentigny, was on his way, and nothing could be done until he arrived.[18]

After another agonizing night, Washington was summoned to deliver Dinwiddie's letter. The French officers, with Repentigny now present, retired to review it and then called Washington and Jacob Van Braam in to verify their understanding. Washington himself read its contents, line by line, slowly, to the French officers before him. Dismissing him, the French officers retied to form a reply. This must have been discouraging.[19]

Washington had waited months for this moment and must have gone over how it would happen dozens of times in his mind during the long, cold miles. Now, the moment was unfolding in a way he had not foreseen; it was slipping away.

While awaiting his host's response, Washington took in the fort. He observed:

> It is situated on the South, or West Fork of French Creek, near the Water, and is almost surrounded by the Creek, and a small Branch of it which forms a Kind of an Island, four Houses compose the Sides, the Bastions are made of Piles driven into the Ground, and about 12 Feet above, and Sharp at Top, with Port-Holes cut for Cannon and Loop-Holes for small

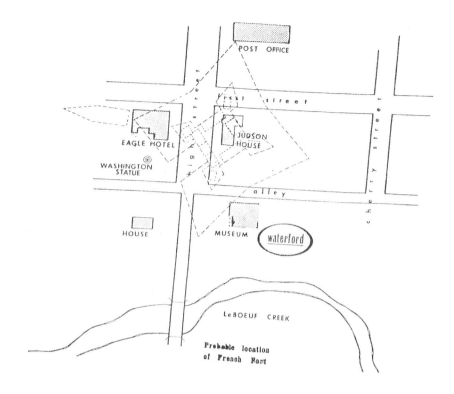

A map showing the site of the fort superimposed on a modern city map. *Fort Le Bouef Historical Society.*

> *Arms to Fire though, there are eight 6 lb. Pieces mounted, two in each Bastion, and one Piece of four Pound before the Gate; in the Bastions are a Guard-House, Chapel, Doctor's Lodging, and the Commander's private Store, round which are laid Plat-Forms for the Cannon and Men to stand on: There are several Barracks without the Fort, for the Soldiers' Dwelling, covered some with Bark, and some with Boards, and made chiefly of Loggs; There are also several other Houses, such as Stables, Smiths Shop, &.*[20]

The next day, December 14, Washington looked after the business of preparing for their return, all the while awaiting the French reply. That evening, it came, not in a face-to-face meeting, but in the form of a sealed letter for Dinwiddie. Washington would not know its contents for another month. It must have eaten at him to carry the letter, unable to read its contents.[21]

A statue of Washington stands in a park across from the Fort LeBeouf Museum. *Author's collection.*

Seeing that their horses were weak and the weather was bad, Washington sent off most of the group and the horses to wait for them at Venango; he and Gist would travel on foot to meet them there. Tanacharison gave the French his wampum, but Saint Pierre refused to receive it, symbolically saying that the French did not hear his message. As they had at Venango, the French plied the Half King and his entourage with gifts, and he wanted to stay and enjoy the hospitality. The French were blatantly trying to lure the Natives away and drive a wedge between them and the Virginians. Washington, with his mission completed, was more than ready to go.[22]

On the return trip, they stopped at the Venango trading post on December 22. The next day, Washington met with Tanacharison, who he was afraid would be tempted to stay by the French with designs to lure him away from the British cause. One of the other Natives was ill, and the Half King insisted they stay behind. Washington left Van Braam to look after the baggage and proceeded with just Gist.[23]

In the bad weather, Washington wore more practical Native clothing, shedding his uniform and European hat and boots. He and Gist camped along Sandy Creek in modern-day Mercer County on Christmas Eve. The day after Christmas, their emaciated horses gave out, and they set out on foot.[24]

At the Native village of Murtheringtown, between modern Zelienople and Evans City, Gist and Washington picked up a guide, a Native they had seen at Venango, to assist them. As the three men made their way south, Washington and Gist grew suspicious of the Native but could not share their thoughts out loud. The Native offered to carry Washington's weapon, which Washington refused, and seemed to lead them in the wrong direction.[25]

When Gist and Washington entered a clearing, the guide was several steps ahead of them. Washington noted in his journal that the Native suddenly turned and fired at them. The Native was "not 15 Steps, but fortunately missed. We took this Fellow into Custody, and kept him till about 9 o'Clock at Night, and then let him go, and walked the remaining part of the Night without making any Stop…as to be out of the Reach of their Pursuit." Had either Gist or Washington been hit, it is likely that neither would have survived in the winter conditions, and Washington would be known only as an obscure colonial officer.[26]

On December 29, the pair reached the north bank of the icy Allegheny River. They constructed a crude raft and made their way across. Losing his balance, Washington fell into frigid water and was rescued by Gist. The two spent the night on an island now known as Hears Island, where the Fortieth Street Bridge crosses the river in Pittsburgh today.[27]

This monument notes the attempted murder of Washington by his Indian scout. *Author's collection.*

Within a twenty-four-hour period, Washington had survived an assassination attempt, a fall into the icy Allegheny River and a night in the freezing cold in wet clothes. He was already under stress from the mission, and he was anxious about the French reply, which he still did not know the details of.

Gist and Washington continued south, making a brief stop at Shannopin's Town, now the site of the Monongahela Wharf parking lot in Pittsburgh, to rest and get food. They also stopped at Frazier's cabin at the mouth of Turtle Creek along the Monongahela River. Then they followed the Nemacolin Path south and east, crossing Chestnut Ridge and Laurel Ridge, to Will's Creek and on to Winchester. There was much to reflect on as they trudged the long, cold miles. They reached Williamsburg on January 11, 1754. After delivering the letter to Governor Dinwiddie at the governor's palace, Washington finally learned its contents. Saint-Pierre's answer to Dinwiddie was short and to the Point:

> *As to the Summons you send me to retire, I do not think myself obliged to obey it; whatever may be your Instructions, I am here by Virtue of the*

Orders of my General; and I intreat you, Sir, not to doubt one Moment, but that I am determin'd to conform myself to them with all the Exactness and Resolution which can be expected from the best Officer.

I have the honor to be,

Sir,
Your very humble and very obedient servant,

Legardeur de Saint-Pierre
From the Fort on the Riviere Aux Boeufs,
December 15, 1753

Dinwiddie was ready to respond with force and ordered the militia to be called out. Recruitment was so slow that the governor then bypassed the militia system and raised a regiment funded by the colony, the Virginia Regiment, to enter the region and occupy the Forks of the Ohio River ahead of the French.[28]

Washington had not only gained valuable frontier experience, but he had also earned a new name, Caunotaucarius, meaning "town taker" or "town destroyer." Apparently, the Half King called him this on their way to Fort Le Boeuf. Decades later, Washington recounted the story, "It was on this occasion he was named by the half-King (as he was called) and the tribes of Nations with whom he treated—Caunotaucarius (in English) the Town-taker; which name being registered in their Manner & communicated to other Nations of Indians, has been remembered by them ever since in all their transactions with him during the late war."[29]

Washington learned that Native diplomacy was a delicate and slow process with its own set of understandings and procedures. The process was based on trust, gifts, speeches and the acknowledgement of previous treaties and relationships. It was entirely foreign to English and French tradition and concepts of diplomacy.

In the race to get to the vital Forks of the Ohio River, the British got there first. On February 17, William Trent, a frontier trader, with forty Virginia militiamen occupied the Point and began constructing a crude fort called Fort Prince George. Trent had experience from King George's War (1746–47) and was the son of the founder of Trenton, New Jersey, who was also a wealthy judge and Philadelphia merchant. A tall man, the younger Trent stood at about six feet tall.[30]

The royal governor's palace in Williamsburg was one of the most impressive buildings in the British colonies. From here, Virginia's leaders projected power across half a continent. *Author's collection.*

At the Point, there was a crisis in leadership among the British. Trent had gone to Wills Creek for supplies. John Frazier, the second-in-command, had gone to his house at Turtle Creek, leaving Ensign Edward Ward in charge of Fort Prince George. It hardly deserved to be called a fort, as it comprised only some upright logs and a storehouse.[31]

On the way to reinforce the tiny garrison at the Forks were troops under the command of Lieutenant Colonel Washington. They were toting several swivel guns (small-caliber artillery guns that could be mounted on a post or wall) and had departed for Wills Creek, leaving Alexandria on April 2. Soon, more troops under the command of Captain Adam Stephen joined them, bringing the total strength to 160 men. It was 220 arduous miles to the Forks of the Ohio River. The men were under the overall command of Colonel Joshua Fry. Would they make it in time?[32]

On April 16, about five hundred French troops under the command of Captain Claude Pierre Pecuady, sieur de Contrecoeur, arrived at the Point, making a show of overwhelming force. Contrecoeur had been on the Celeron expedition and previously commanded Fort Niagara. The French, complete with artillery, landed on the shore of la Belle Riviere and marched toward the Point. The next day, they marched within musket shot of Ward's thirty-three Virginians in their makeshift fort.[33]

The French sent a message indicating that the English were trespassing on French territory, and they requested that they leave—not unlike Dinwiddie's message. Facing overwhelming numbers, Ward agreed, and the French set noon the next day as their time to depart. Seeing the Virginians were low on supplies, Contercoeur gave them food for their journey back to Wills Creek.[34]

The incident was not without some drama, as Tanacharison was visibly upset at the feebleness of the English. After all, he had staked his reputation and the fortunes of the Ohio Natives on the English, and they now appeared to be losing in the growing struggle. According to Ward, the Half King "stormed greatly at the French at the time they were obliged to march out of the Fort and told them it was he Odere'd that fort and laid the first log of it himself." The French "paid no regard to what he said." It was a clear snub that indicated his irrelevance.[35]

Immediately, the French tore down the English fort and began building a proper fortification, Fort Duquesne. According to English prisoner John McKinney, who was held at the fort in 1756, Fort Duquesne was square with bastions about fifty yards long and about forty yards wide. It had half square logs on the land side and only a wooden stockade on the water side, where less strength was needed. There were two gates on the land side and one on the water side. The land side also had a drawbridge. The fort's bastions were filled with earth and stood eight feet tall. Each bastion had four gun carriages. Outside the fort, Natives camped, coming and going with the seasons.[36]

In the meantime, Washington's column made slow progress, reaching Wills Creek on April 21, unaware that the French had taken the Point. The next day, Ensign Ward and his defeated troops arrived from the Forks. Continuing on to retake the Point, Washington had his troops improve Nemacolin's Path to accommodate the wagons and troops over the mountains. The English and French had not yet come to blows, but now, both groups had sent troops into the region. War was on the horizon.[37]

Fort Duquesne was nearly six hundred miles from Montreal at the far end of a long and tenuous supply line that passed over lakes and along rivers, subject to the weather and enemy raids. The French faced other disadvantages, too. The growing season in New France was much shorter than the growing season in the southern English colonies, and being able to supply enough food was always a challenge for the Canadiens, even in peaceful years without milice call-ups. The population of New France was also much smaller, and the Canadiens were outnumbered by the English colonists twenty-five to one.

The more populated English settlements also sat squarely between New France and Europe, meaning all French supplies and reinforcements had to sail past English territory to reach Quebec. New France's ports were also iced in for many months of the year, while most of the English harbors were ice-free year-round.[38]

Yet the French had advantages that were by no means insignificant. New France was ruled by one governor, who could act swiftly and decisively. The various English colonies had long-standing rivalries that undercut their efforts. Divided by religion and culture—and often in competition for western land—the English colonies were rarely united in their efforts and were often slow to act, as they had to coordinate with each other and the Crown. The English also had fewer Native allies.

As tensions heated up in the Ohio Country, conflict was inevitable. Among the Delaware, Shawnee and Mingo, the elders could not remember a time when a crisis of such magnitude confronted them. Their ancestors had been driven from the east, and here, they faced encroachment again. No one could agree on what course to take or how to help their people survive.

Sites to Explore

Fort Le Boeuf Museum
103 South High Street | Waterford, PA 16641
814-796-4014 | www.fortleboeufhistory.com/campus/museum
GPS: 41 56.405, -79 58.952

This fort was visited by Washington on his mission to warn the French to leave the Ohio Country, and the museum that now occupies it interprets the little-known French invasion of the region. The operation was a massive undertaking that required large numbers of supplies and delicate Native diplomacy. Directly across the street is George Washington Memorial Park.

Fort Machault/Fort Venango Markers

The Native town of Venango is where John Frazier built a trading post that was appropriated by the French in 1753. Washington stopped here on his way to Fort Le Boeuf. Later, the French built Fort Machault on the site, and after the war, the British occupied the land and built Fort Venango.

The sites of these forts are gone, and there is no historic site or museum there today. Two historic markers stand at the intersection of Eighth Street (U.S. 322) and Elk Street in Franklin, Pennsylvania (GPS: 41 23.359, 79 49.33).

GEORGE WASHINGTON
MEMORIAL PARK
THE CORNER OF FIRST ALLEY
AND SOUTH HIGH STREETS
WATERFORD, PA
GPS: 41 56.4, -79 58.977

A cluster of historic markers note Washington's visit and the forts that once stood here. There is also a statue of the young messenger here. They are all across the street from the Fort Le Boeuf Museum. There are no facilities at this site.

Across the street from the site of the fort is a park with several markers about Washington's visit. Author's collection.

GUYASUTA STATUE
LOCATED AT THE INTERSECTION OF MAIN STREET
AND NORTH CANAL STREET
H.J. HEINZ MEMORIAL PLAZA, PITTSBURGH, PA 15215
GPS: 40 29.678, -79 55.937

This leader of the Seneca guided Washington on his 1753 survey of the Point. He later commanded the Native forces at the Battle of Bushy Run in 1763. There are no facilities at this site.

HERR'S ISLAND MARKER
THREE RIVERS HERITAGE TRAIL
GPS: 40 27.579, -79 58.967

Washington and Gist crossed the icy Allegheny River here. At one point, Washington fell in and had to be rescued by Gist. This marker is located just west of the entrance of the pedestrian bridge to Herr's Island.

Logstown Markers

Logstown/Legionville Historic Park and Center, Baden, PA 15005
GPS: 40 37.372, -80 13.592

Several historical markers stand at the intersection of Duss Avenue and Anthony Wayne Drive. From 1727 to 1758, this was one of the largest Native towns in the region. Several important conferences took place here. Washington visited in 1753.

Point of View Monument
Intersection of Grandview Avenue and Sweetbriar Street
Pittsburgh, PA

This sculpture depicts Washington and Seneca chief Guyasuta, who met in October 1770. The statue commemorates a pivotal moment, with the past and future gazing at each other above the Forks of the Ohio River. There are no facilities at this site.

Washington Assassination Monument
Pennsylvania Route 68, 0.1 miles North of Ash Stop Road
Evans City, PA 16033
GPS: 40 47.295, -80 1.95

This stone monument claims to mark the site where a hostile Indian tried to kill Washington and Gist on their return from Fort Machault on December 27, 1753. There are no facilities at this site.

Washington's Trail
www.washingtonstrail.org

This website has information about Washington sites from the 1753 expedition and useful information to be able to follow the route today.

Washington's Trail markers like these note the route of the young officer across western Maryland and Pennsylvania on his 1753 diplomatic mission. *Author's collection.*

4

FORT NECESSITY

A Charming Field.
—*George Washington describing the battlefield*

In the spring of 1754, the French had completed their occupation of the Ohio Country; they had removed the British from the Forks of the Ohio River and begun building Fort Duquesne. Among those who began arriving there was twenty-one-year-old Frenchman Charles Bonin, who possessed a "desire for travel." He volunteered for service in New France and found himself assigned to the artillery. On his way from Montreal to la Belle Riviere, Bonin viewed the falls at Niagara, where he noted that the ground trembled and he was soaked by the mist. He was first stationed at Fort De la Presque Isle, and then he was sent to Fort Duquesne.[1]

Bonin described the fort at la Belle Riviere: "The fort was built of squared timbers twelve feet thick on the land side; its thickness filled with earth; with a strong parapet; and three bastions each mounting four cannon. It had a deep moat on the outside and a drawbridge on the north." A drawbridge provided access to the fort over the moat from the east. Inside were a bakehouse, a guardhouse, barracks, officers' quarters and a storehouse.[2]

The French built the strongest walls on the land sides, as any attack was likely to come by land. The western, or water-facing, sides were built simply using a palisade of upright logs. Every spring, the rivers flooded and parts of the fort became submerged, so the French chose to construct a palisade in those areas, as it was easier to repair than earthen walls.

With Fort Duquesne established (it was not completed until late summer), the French could exert their influence on the tribes of the Ohio Country. It became a center of trade and diplomacy between the French and the Ohio Country Natives, as well as Natives from farther away. The garrison included a few women, and several children were born and baptized at the fort.

The French also actively gathered intelligence about British intentions in the region. To that end, Contrecoeur dispatched a force of about thirty-three soldiers under Ensign Joseph Coulon de Jumonville to the southeast, toward the road (Nemacolin's Trail) that the Virginians were building. Jumonville was a lifelong soldier and had six brothers who also served in the Compagnies Frances de la Marine. He had a great deal of frontier experience, as he had been posted at sites from Louisiana to the Illinois Country.[3]

Contrecoeur recorded that Jumonville was to find whether the English were in French territory, and if they were, he was to deliver the summons. His instructions also noted that he was, "before making the summons, to send us a good pair of legs in order to inform us about what he has learned on the day he expects to make the summons." So, before making contact with the English, Jumonville was to send a runner back to inform Contrecoeur at Fort Duquesne.[4]

Point State Park in downtown Pittsburgh, the objective of both the French and the British. The Allegheny River (*left*) meets the Monongahela River (*right*) to form the massive Ohio River. In the center is the outline of Fort Duquesne, and in the upper right corner is the reconstructed wall of Fort Pitt. *Author's collection.*

Moving west from Wills Creek on April 30, Washington's force of 160 followed the 1752 path laid out by Gist; they widened it and crossed the high ridges of western Maryland. The Virginians crossed the Casselman River at a ford known as Little Crossings and then moved over what would be the Mason-Dixon line before passing over the Youghiogheny River at Great Crossings.[5]

By early May, Washington's force had met several traders who reported on the French building Fort Duquesne and on French efforts to convert the Natives to their cause. In the coming days, more traders passed by, as they were abandoning the area for fear of the French.[6]

Looking for an easier way west—and avoiding the imposing heights of Laurel Ridge—Washington hoped to use the water route of the Youghiogheny River. The river's name, a Lenape word, means "a stream flowing in a contrary direction," a reference to the many twists and turns the river makes before entering the Monongahela River. Yet on May 20, when Washington and four men took to their canoes in the river, they found the falls at Ohiopyle. This Lenape word means "white, frothy, water." The river drops sixty feet over one mile and has a forty-six-foot-tall waterfall. With this obstacle, Washington returned to building the road west from the Great Meadows.[7]

On May 24, Washington and his Virginia regiment arrived at a large natural clearing bisected by a swampy stream that is known as the Great Meadows. It was a pleasing landmark and a place to rest after crossing the mountains and fording the Youghiogheny River at Great Crossings. After he arrived, Washington received reports from friendly Natives and a local trader who dealt with the French troops in the area.[8]

Tanacharison and Scaroudy, the two Half Kings who represented the Iroquois, brought a small number of Iroquois warriors to Washington's camp at Great Meadows. The Natives were curious to see how the English would proceed.[9]

On May 27, Washington wrote, "Mr. Gist arrived early in the morning, who told us that Mr. LaForce, with fifty men whose tracks he had seen five miles from here, had been at his plantation the day before." Gist's plantation was about twelve miles to the north at the foot of Chestnut Ridge, near modern-day Connellsville.[10]

In the meantime, the Virginians worked on a fortification at the Great Meadow and eventually built a simple palisade of upright logs around a storehouse, with trenches in front and swivel guns mounted in the trenches. Reports from traders and friendly Natives continued to pour in. By late May,

Washington knew that a force under the command of Jumonville had been sent from Fort Duquesne, but their purpose was not clear. Washington's journal states that they were sent to "capture and kill all the English they might find."[11]

Around eight o'clock on the evening of May 27, a Native sent by Tancharrrison arrived to report that he had found a French force hidden in a nearby glen. With forty men, Washington set out to link up with the Half King and attack (although only thirty-three men made it to the Half King's camp). It was an unpleasant march to say the least. Washington recalled that the march was done in "a heavy rain, and in a night as dark as pitch, along a path scarce broad enough for one man; we were sometimes fifteen or twenty minutes out of the path before we could come on it again, and we would often strike against each other in the darkness. All night long we continued our route, and on the 28th about sun-rise we arrived at the Indian camp."[12]

Tanacharison was waiting at what has become known as Half King's Rock, a large outcropping at the crest of Laurel Ridge, north of where modern-day Route 40 intersects with Jumonville Road. Together, the forces set out to find the French. The conditions were horrible, and the men were exhausted, as they had already been working hard and were low on rations. Washington was physically tired and mentally drained, and he lacked good intelligence about the force ahead or their intentions.[13]

With thirty-three troops and twelve Natives, Washington and the Half King divided their forces and surrounded the French at the rocky outcropping that has since been known as Jumonville Glen. The French had no sentries on duty—either a poor oversight or a reflection of their diplomatic mission. Captain Adam Stephen, with about twenty men, approached from the west and waited on the crest overlooking the French camp. Washington himself led another twenty men directly against the camp from the south and east. Tanacharison and his Natives sealed off escape from the north.[14]

It was about seven or eight o'clock in the morning; the French were cooking breakfast when they looked up and saw Washington's group approaching. A recently discovered Native account from the UK National Archives reveals that Washington himself fired the first shot. The French tried to form up but were hit by fire from the front and behind.[15]

There was no doubt in Washington's mind about the intentions of the French—or about his own intentions. He approached the French camp with the intention to attack, not scout or parley. It was over in about fifteen minutes. Thirteen Frenchmen were killed, and twenty-one were taken

Jumonville Glen was the site of George Washington's very first battle. Today, it is part of the Fort Necessity National Battlefield. French troops were camped among the massive boulders when they were surrounded and surprised by Virginia militia and their Native allies. *Author's collection.*

prisoner. One Virginian was killed, and two or three wounded. There were no Native casualties.

Tanacharison stood over the wounded Jumonville, who attempted to read his summons. Ironically, it was a similar message to the one Washington had delivered to the French six months earlier: the territory was theirs, and they requested that the English leave. Before he could finish reading his message, Tanacharison stepped up and said, "Tu n'es pas encore mort, mon pere." ("You are not yet dead, my father."). He then split Jumonvilles's skull open with his tomahawk.[16]

Washington wrote afterward that the French claimed to have called out to read the summons when the firing began. He called this "an absolute falsehood," noting that he was at the head of the attacking force and saw them getting their weapons to defend themselves.[17]

One Canadien soldier escaped the ambush, as he had gone into the woods to answer the call of nature. Mouceau (records do not indicate his full name) made his way, barefoot and without provisions, sixty miles back to Fort Duquesne to report on what had happened. The Virginians did not know of his escape, but it would be crucial.[18]

Back at Fort Duquesne, Monceau relayed to Contrecoeur:

> *In the morning, at seven o'clock, they found they were surrounded by English on one side and Indians on the other. They received two volleys from the English and not from the Indians. Through an interpreter M. de Jumonville then told them to stop, as he had to speak to them. They stopped. M. de Jumonville had the summons read to them, my summons for them to retire....While it was being read, the said Monceau saw all our Frenchmen coming up behind M. de Jumonville, so that they formed a platoon in the midst of the English and the Indians. Meanwhile, Monceau slipped to one side, and went off through the woods.*[19]

Contrecoeur heard from Natives that Jumonville had been killed while relaying the summons—he had been shot in the head. This secondhand account is probably erroneous. It at least mixes up the facts. A French officer named Drouillon was taken prisoner, and from his captivity, he wrote to Governor Dinwiddie insisting that they were on a diplomatic mission. Drouillon noted that the French did not take up their arms when Washington attacked and that they called out to parley. Yet Washington stated that the French ran to their weapons when the fighting started.[20]

The French clearly returned fire, as there were English casualties. Captain Adam Stephen also stated that the French fired back and in fact notes that their weapons and powder were dry. Meanwhile, the Virginians had been marching the rain, and their weapons were in worse condition. He makes no mention of a call to parley.[21]

It is worth noting that the two French accounts, those of Monceau and Drouillon, do not agree. Monceau noted that Jumonville halted the firing and began reading the summons. Drouillon, in writing to Dinwiddie, said that the French called out to Washington. In making his case to the Virginia governor, Drouillon was surely trying to put the French in the best light as diplomats.[22]

Perhaps all accounts are true to a degree, as the limited vision of the witnesses could have influenced them. The Jumonville affair is one of the most muddied events of the entire conflict. We will likely never know what really happened that rainy morning in the glen. In 2023, National Park Service archaeologists investigated the battle site, confirming its location and recovering several musket balls and other artifacts. It was the first time archaeology had been conducted at the site.

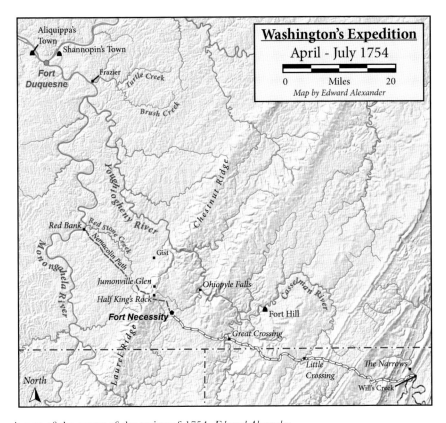

A map of the events of the spring of 1754. *Edward Alexander.*

This was George Washington's first battle, and it was a success, but certainly, in the days afterward, he reflected on what he had done. He had attacked an enemy force, not knowing their intentions. In his letters afterward to Dinwiddie, Washington maintained that the French party was spying and intending to attack his force. Washington pointed out that the French had lain hidden in the glen for several days. If they were diplomats on a mission to deliver a message—as he had done—why wait? Were they spying on the British?[23]

Jumonville left Fort Duquesne on May 23 and was ambushed on May 28. They journeyed down the Monongahela River to Red Stone Creek and then marched east. At most, it would have taken him two days to reach Chestnut Ridge. His force was camped in the glen for several days without making contact with the English at Great Meadows, just a few miles away. Why? French officer Drouillin said that they arrived on May 26 and that they did not know how close they were to the English.[24]

Washington may have been swayed by Tanacharison, who had clearly thrown his lot with the English and could not afford to lose face. The elderly Native chief might have pushed the young Washington to attack.

Of course, Jumonville was dead and could not explain his intentions. If the French were spying, planning to attack or had otherwise hostile intentions, why did they not post guards? Their camp was not set up for any kind of defense, with their backs to the steep rock wall. This was not the behavior of a force expecting to meet an enemy.

Sometimes, diplomacy and espionage went hand in hand, as Washington's journey the year before illustrates. He courted the Natives and attempted to gain their allegiance, and he made notes of the French fortifications. The French made overt efforts to lure the Natives away from his party. Historians ever since have debated whether the French were on a purely diplomatic mission or if they were there to spy and possibly attack. Maybe both? We will likely never know for sure.[25]

Returning to the Great Meadows, Washington oversaw the construction of a storage cabin and a stockade and received more Native visitors at the camp. He sent the French prisoners to Winchester under guard. Washington wrote to his brother Augustine about the battle: "I fortunately escaped without any wound, for the right wing, where I stood, was exposed to and received all the enemy's fire, and it was the part where the man was killed, and the rest wounded. I heard the bullet whistle, and believe me, there is something charming in the sound."[26]

On June 1, Queen Aliquippa and about eighty-five refugees, including many women and children, arrived at the camp in the Great Meadows. These Seneca had abandoned their town close to Fort Duquesne. Now that it seemed battle lines had been drawn, the Natives were choosing sides. Over the next few days, Tanacharison and Washington debated their strategy. The old sachem insisted that the log fort, which Washington had named Fort Necessity, would not stand up to an attack. The young officer disagreed, insisting it was the place to make a stand for the French response that was sure to come.[27]

On June 4, a Native arrived who had been at Fort Duquesne when Mouceau stumbled in and told the garrison of the fate of Jumonville and his party. Now, Washington and the Half King knew that the French had learned of the attack, and they knew the French response would be swift. A few days prior, nine French deserters arrived at Fort Necessity. They told Washington that more Natives, including the Delaware and Shawnee, were joining the French. From his interview with them, Washington was

Fort Necessity stood in the lowest part of the Great Meadows, with high ground all around it. Today, a reconstructed fort is on this exact site. *Author's collection.*

reaffirmed in his assessment that Jumonville's party was sent to either spy on or attack his force.[28]

If Washington was feeling anxious, his mood could not have improved with the next piece of news to arrive: Colonel Joshua Fry had fallen off his horse and died at Wills Creek. Washington alone was now in charge. Reinforcements soon arrived, but they were not a blessing.

On June 14, Captain James Mackay arrived with the independent company from South Carolina. These were armed and trained British regulars, but as a regular officer, Captain Mackay outranked the colonial colonel Washington. Mackay refused to take orders from Washington and insisted that they command jointly. Furthermore, his regular troops would do no manual labor; thus, the Virginians were left to finish the fortifications while the regulars watched. The quality of these troops remains in doubt, as prior to their arrival, they had seen hard service on the Carolina frontier and were in need of new weapons before their journey north.[29]

The British military stationed independent companies throughout the colonies. These small units were stationed in the various colonies and could be sent where needed, as they were not attached to organized regiments. Governor Dinwiddie had requested that several independent companies that were stationed in other colonies be sent to join the Virginia Regiment. The troops from South Carolina were the only ones who arrived by June.

Washington had learned enough of frontier warfare to effectively use his Native allies. Scouts were constantly reporting on the French and the situation among various tribes. Yet all was not well at Great Meadows. Supplies were low, and the French at Fort Duquesne heavily outnumbered them. Most of the Delaware, Shawnee, Wyandot and Mingo had departed with Tanacharison, and only a handful remained by late June.[30]

There was a great deal of unhappiness among the troops as well. John Shaw, a soldier from Virginia, wrote that at one point, they had gone several days with only a quart of corn for food. Combined with the physical work of building the road and the fort, the men were weak and exhausted. In fact, by the end of June, most of the army's flour and bacon, the staples of their rations, was gone. Shaw also noted issues with pay.[31]

Washington wrote to Governor Dinwiddie, "We have with Natures assistance made a good Intrenchment, and by clearing ye Bushes out of these Meadows prear'd a charming field for an Encounter." Fort Necessity, by this time, was as finished as it could be. The fort was a round stockade of upright logs (palisade) with a small storehouse inside. On either side of the fort were trenches, and two of the swivel guns were mounted there.[32]

It was a terrible place to make a stand. The round stockade could hold only about sixty men inside; the rest had to use the shallow, muddy trenches. Roaming beyond the trenches, among some tents and wagons, were the few cows that were still left. The fort was located in the low part of the meadow on marshy ground, and it would soon flood with the coming rain. There was no natural cover for the Virginians. On three sides, high ground and wilderness overlooked the fort, providing natural cover for an enemy.[33]

Private Shaw described the fort as "a Small Stocado Fort made in a Circular fform round a Small House that Stood in the Middle of it to keep our provisions and Ammunition in, And was Cover'd with Bark and some Skins, and might be about fourteen ffeet Square, and the Walls of the Fort might be eight ffeet Distance from the said House all Round."[34]

The fort's problems were numerous: there were few proper tools, the force occupying it was small and the troops were weak from lack of rations. Why was Washington drawn to the Great Meadows, and why did he insist that he make his stand there, even against the advice of his Native allies? As it was

Swivel guns like this were portable and easy to transport on the frontier. The French insisted that Washington surrender his swivel guns as part of the capitulation. *Author's collection.*

one of few clearings in the area, perhaps a break from the threatening woods appealed to someone used to settled areas.

Altogether, Washington and Mackay commanded about four hundred troops. The French and Native force coming toward them included about six hundred French and Canadiens and about one hundred Natives. There is no concrete evidence on the number of French troops. They were led by Captain Sieur Louis Coulon de Villiers, the brother of Jumonville. He was born near Montreal along the St. Lawrence River. Forty-five years old that year, de Villiers had extensive experience at frontier posts in La Bye (modern-day Green Bay, Wisconsin) as well as other assignments in the far-western Illinois Country.[35]

Anxious to avenge the loss of his brother, de Villiers stopped at the site of the ambush in the glen a month afterward and found the bodies unburied. They buried the remains properly and moved on to face the British. On July 3, the French and Native force approached the Great Meadows. De Villiers wrote in his report that as his troops closed in on the fort, "some of my people returned to tell me that we were discovered; and that the English approached in order of battle to attack us."[36]

The French, de Villiers admitted, "were not acquitted with the ground," so as they approached, they "presented our flank to the fort from whence they began to cannonade us." On their right, the English approached "in order of battle." De Villiers noted that the English very quickly withdrew into their fortifications. "We then set ourselves about investing the fort: it was advantageously enough situated in a meadow, the wood of which was within musket shot of it. We came as close to them as it was possible…the fire was pretty brisk on both sides." The French surrounded the fort to cut off any chance of escape.[37]

Bonin reported:

> *We advanced in three columns to the right. All the savages went to the left, shouting the war cry, which so frightened the fifty leaving the fort that they turned back hastily. We advanced opposite the fort, but only within rifle shot, because the fort was built in the middle of the plain. We had scarcely arrived in this position when the fort's cannon began to fire on us with grapeshot (they were small cannons). We were in the woods, each behind a tree. As we had no cannon, we could only return fire with rifle shots. We nevertheless, reached the fort.*
>
> *Our musketry-fire lasted until eight o'clock in the evening, when we sent an officer with a drummer to summon the commander to surrender, failing which they would be taken by assault.*
>
> *Actually we had been preparing for this by making fascines during the firing. This precaution was unnecessary because at the very moment when the officer bearing the summons was going toward the fort, the enemy's flag was lowered.*[38]

Washington noted that "finding they had no Intention of attacking us in the open Field, we retired into our Trenches." He waited for the French to assault directly, which made no sense given their superior position from the woods and high ground around the fort. After the assault never came, he ordered his defenders to fire.[39]

A secondhand account of the battle recorded by Virginia landowner Landon Carter notes that Lieutenant Colonel George Muse, Washington's second-in-command, "Instead of bringing up the 2^d division to make the Attack with the first, he marched them or rather frightened them back to the trenches, so that the Colo. at the head of the Carolina independent company was greatly exposed to the French Fire and were forced to retire to the same trenches, where they were galled on All sides." It is unclear how Carter received his information, but it is possible he got it from a participant.[40]

George Washington was a young Virginia militia officer who aspired to a career in the British military. *Library of Congress.*

Did Lieutenant Colonel George Muse pull his troops back to the trenches without orders? Was it a mistake? Washington wrote that he pulled back on purpose, but Carter's account makes it seem like Muse's action forced Washington's hand. It ultimately mattered little, since the French were not going to fight in the open and would have taken to the trees eventually.

The French and Natives could get within sixty yards of the fort in the cover of the woods to fire on the defenders. The Virginians by contrast, were trapped and could not see their targets as they fired back. Then the skies opened up. Muskets fouled, and cartridges became unusable in the rain. The hands and faces of the British were smeared with powder from loading and firing in the downpour. Everything in and around the fort was in range, as even the dogs, cattle and horses could be picked off with impunity. Water filled the trenches.

Private Shaw of Virginia noted, "The ffrench were at that time so near that Severall of our people were wounded by the Splinters beat off by the Bulletts from the said House." Miserable in their situation, some of the British broke into the rum supply and began to get drunk and unmanageable. Darkness descended, and the rain continued.[41]

De Villiers noted later, "The enemy's fire began again at six o'clock, with more fury than ever, and lasted till eight o'clock." According to Washington, the French were "sheltered behind the Trees, ourselves without Shelter, in Trenches full of Water, in a settled Rain, and the Enemy galling us on all Sides incessantly from the Woods." At this point, the French called out and asked to parley.[42]

Not wanting the French to come into his lines and see the appalling condition of his troops, Washington sent Van Bramm and another who spoke French, William La Peronie, to meet with the French outside the fort. La Peronie was injured in the battle, and due to loss of blood, he was unable to continue with the negotiations, leaving it all to the Dutchman Van Bramm to translate from French to English.[43]

He returned with two copies of rain-soaked surrender terms. If he accepted, Washington was to indicate by not raising his flag in morning. In the fort's storehouse, Washington described looking over the document by the light of a candle. As he could scarcely see it—and it was in French—he had to take Van Braam's word for it. Both Mackay and Washington signed the "wet and blotted paper."[44]

Unknown to him at the time, the surrender document Washington signed accused him of assassinating the commander of the earlier French detachment he had ambushed. Apparently, Van Braam misinterpreted the word. Washington maintained that he did not assassinate a diplomat and that in signing the document he was unaware of the charge.

Washington later blamed Van Braam for missing such a crucial point. It could have been an innocent mistake, as Jumonville was killed by Tanchraison. Or was it just glossed over it in the poor conditions? Washington and Mackay certainly would have objected to the admission of assassinating Jumonville had they known. Today, the original document resides in the archives in Montreal.[45]

As the sun came up on Thursday, July 4, no flag rose above the stockade. French troops then marched up, and the Natives gathered to watch. The British marched out with the honors of war, a military custom that allowed them to beat their drums and take their weapons with them.

The articles of surrender specified that the British would leave two hostages with the French, and Jacob Van Bramm and Captain Robert Stobo of Virginia were chosen. They were to be held until the French prisoners who were taken at Jumonville Glen were returned. Stobo would spend his captivity at Fort Duquesne examining the fort and smuggling a map out (with the help of a Native known as Delaware George), which eventually reached British forces in Virginia.[46]

The letter was captured in General Edward Braddock's baggage the following year. As punishment, Stobo was sent to Quebec, tried and sentenced to death. Yet he escaped and returned to Virginia. He continued his army career and rose to the rank of captain in the Fifth Regiment of Foot. On June 19, 1775 (just a month after the Battles of Lexington and Concord), he killed himself with his service pistol, perhaps haunted by what he had seen and experienced on the frontier.[47]

One final incident unfolded before the defeated British marched away. Captain Adam Stephen was told that a French soldier had taken his portmanteau, a leather traveling bag. He spotted the soldier as he made his way toward a crowd of French troops, so Stephen pursued. He grabbed the portmanteau, kicked the soldier and began to walk back to British lines.

Some French officers saw the incident and stepped up to investigate. Stephen was covered in mud and without his proper uniform. They asked if he was an officer, and he affirmed; then he pulled out his regimental uniform to show them. A lowly British private would have been scolded by the French officers, but a fellow officer deserved respect, so they let him go.[48]

The British then departed for the march back to Wills Creek. Fort Necessity was the only time in Washington's military career that he surrendered. His defeat also came at the hands of the French while in service to the British. Two decades later, he defeated the British with the help of the French. It was also July 4. Washington reflected on these ironies later in life, including in a letter to then Continental officer Adam Stephen in 1776.[49]

De Villiers noted, "I sent a detachment to take possession of the fort; the garrison filed off, and the number of their dead and wounded raised compassion in me, notwithstanding my resentment of the manner in which they had made away with my brother." He continues, "The consternation of the English was so great that they ran away and left behind them even their flag and a pair of their colors. I demolished their fort and Mr. le Mercier caused the cannon to be destroyed together with the one which had been granted them by their capitulation, the English not being able to take it away."[50]

The French also destroyed a cask of liquor before departing. De Villiers noted that he had to restrain his Natives from pillaging the English supplies. He noted his losses as two Frenchmen and one Native killed and fifteen Frenchmen and two Natives wounded.[51]

Washington recalled that thirty of his men were killed and seventy were wounded out of about four hundred, a loss of one-fourth of his command. While evacuating the fort, they could not take their provisions for the march back to Wills Creek because of their lack of horses and wagons. Thus, the muddy, weary and hungry British marched out with as much as they could carry for the fifty-mile trek.[52]

Putting the best light on a disastrous performance, Washington wrote that he believed the enemy's loss "must be very considerable." His description also downplays the surrender, noting that "we agreed that each Side should retire without Molestation, they back to their Fort...and we to Will's Creek."[53]

Tanacharison later reflected on the young Washington's leadership:

> *The Colonel was a good-natured man, but had no experience, that he took upon him to command the Indians as his slaves, and would have them every day upon the Out Scout, and attack the Enemy by themselves, and*

that he would by no means take the advice of the Indians that he lay at one place from one full moon to another, and make no fortifications at all but that little thing upon the meadow, where he thought the French could come up to him in the open field; that had he taken the Half King's advice and made such fortifications as the Half King advised him to make, he certainly would have beat the French off.[54]

Tanacharison died on October 7 (there is uncertainty about where he died), well aware of the trouble his people faced but not knowing how it would all turn out.

Washington's journal is an important source when trying to gain the Virginia perspective, but it has an interesting history. The French captured the young officer's journal and translated it, publishing it in Paris two years later. It was then republished in English in London and New York in 1757. Washington first learned of all this and saw the translated journal that year. Unfortunately, the original no longer exists.[55]

This naturally raises the question of how accurate the French translation was, given that the journal covers the incident at Jumonville Glen and the Battle at Great Meadows. Washington himself, upon seeing a published copy, wrote, "I find them as certainly and strangely metamorphosed, some parts left out, which I remember were entered, and many things added that never were thought of.…And the whole of what I saw Englished is very Incorrect and nonsensical; yet, I will not pretend to say that the little body…has not made a literal translation, and a good one." What are we to make of this?[56]

The issue is muddied by the fact that another French translation made in Quebec has survived. This copy was sent to Contrecoeur, the commander at Fort Duquesne. It is noted that it is an extract of Washington's journal. The accompanying letter from Duquesne to Contrecoeur suggests that the writings are an important source of information on Washington's thinking and the British strategy; thus, it is unlikely that it was altered for use as propaganda. The fact that Duquesne accepted it as authentic and sent it to his commander on the frontier to use reinforces the fact that it was a translation done with all good intentions.[57]

Washington must have certainly been horrified to find his writings were not only captured but published by the enemy. Perhaps the French filled in the gaps if his writing was hurried and incomplete. The saga of Washington's 1754 journal, which traveled more than he ever did in his lifetime, is another fascinating aspect of the campaign.[58]

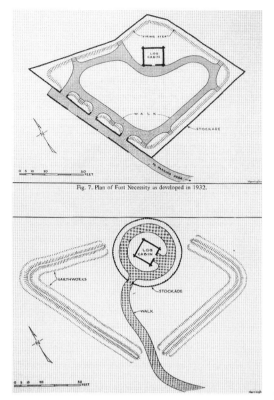

Fig. 7. Plan of Fort Necessity as developed in 1932.

The original understanding of Fort Necessity was based on archaeological studies from the 1930s. Later archaeology found the remains of the circular stockade and understood the trenches to be the outer defenses. *National Park Service.*

De Villiers was knighted in Quebec in 1757 for his service in the Ohio Country. A smallpox epidemic broke out in the city that fall, and he died there in November. Who knows what further contributions he could have made to the French war effort?[59]

The battlefield at the Great Meadows has been the site of commemorations since the 1800s. In 1854, local residents held a July 4 celebration there and intended to place a monument at the site (but this was not done). The battlefield saw gatherings over the years until, in 1926, a chapter of the Sons of the American Revolution formed and pushed for the creation of a military park at the site.[60]

Working with other local patriotic groups, like the Daughters of the American Revolution, the Sons formed a commission to promote the preservation of the battlefield. In 1931, the War Department agreed to study the site, and a military park was created the following year. The movement to preserve the site was part of a wave of patriotism that swept the nation in the 1920s and '30s. In fact, the call was for a "national shrine or memorial" at the site, indicating the reverence held for Washington. Today, it is a National Park.[61]

Archaeologists found the remains of the fort's palisade, showing evidence of burning. This confirmed that the fort was a small circular stockade, setting to rest decades of uncertainty. *National Park Service.*

Washington never gave details about the fort's construction or drew a map of it. A visitor in 1816 recorded surface features that he interpreted to be the ruins of the fort, beginning a long argument about the shape of the structure. The first map of Fort Necessity, based on the 1818 survey, showed a triangular-shaped fort.[62]

In 1830, another inspection of the site produced a drawing that showed a diamond-shaped fort, noting the remains of mounds that must have been the walls of the structure. In 1933, the War Department, having acquired the site, conducted an archaeological study and reconstructed a diamond-shaped stockade fort based on the previous research and the remains of the mounds in the meadow.[63]

A 1952 archaeological survey revealed that what had been interpreted as the fort walls were actually the outlying trenches, and within them was a round stockade of upright logs. Archaeologists found the burned remnants of the posts. A more accurate fort was then reconstructed.[64]

After the French were driven from the Ohio Country, the storehouse at Wills Creek was now the forward base for Virginia. On September 12, 1754, the construction of a fort at the site began on the steep hill overlooking the junction of Wills Creek and the Potomac River. Colonel James Innes oversaw the work with independent companies from New York and South Carolina. By Christmas, the fort was completed, and Innes named it Fort Mount Pleasant.[65]

The fort would be enlarged over the winter and spring of 1755, and it was then renamed Fort Cumberland. The stockade was 400 feet long and 160 feet wide. It was a substantial complex, with four bastions, twenty-seven barracks, a hospital and various storehouses. The soldiers dug a well 80 feet deep to supply the fort with water. The French had now met the English threat and seemed secure in the Ohio Country. Yet the Virginians and the British were not ready to quit so easily.[66]

Sites to Explore

Allegany Museum
3 Pershing Street | Cumberland, MD 21502
301-777-7200 | www.alleganymuseum.org
GPS: 39.650401, -78.762102

Located in downtown Cumberland, this museum covers all aspects of local history, including the French and Indian War.

Casselman River Bridge State Park (Little Crossings Site)
10240 National Pike | Grantsville, MD 21536
GPS: 39 41.802, -79 8.643

The crossing of the Casselman River near Grantsville, Maryland, was known as the Little Crossings, as opposed to the Great Crossings of the Youghiogheny River. Washington's and Braddock's armies crossed here on the Nemacolin Path. Later, a massive stone bridge was built to accommodate the National Road. There are no facilities at this site.

Fort Cumberland Site
218 Washington Street | Cumberland, MD 21502
GPS: 39 39.053, -78 45.935

There is no park or museum here, but the outline of the fort is marked on the ground at the Emmanuel Episcopal Church in Cumberland, Maryland. Nearby is a log structure that was used by Washington during the war and afterward in the Whiskey Rebellion.

Fort Cumberland sat on the high ground (*left*), where the church now stands. *Author's collection.*

There are several historic markers marking the fort on Washington Street and Cherry Place. Underneath the church are the well and powder magazine. Contact the church for tours. There are no facilities at this site.

Washington's Headquarters
38 Greene Street | Cumberland, MD 25102
GPS: 39 38.975, -78 45.885

This log cabin was built in 1755 and used in 1758 by Washington. He also used it briefly in 1794 while reviewing troops as the commander in chief during the Whiskey Rebellion. The cabin is located in Riverside Park, but it originally stood about two blocks away at 16 Washington Street.

Of interest nearby is the Chesapeake and Ohio Canal National Historical Park Visitor Center, which has exhibits on the canal and the National Road, as well as the Western Maryland Scenic Railroad. The Great Allegheny Passage Rail Trail also begins here at the Western Maryland Railroad Station, across the creek from these two sites.

Washington's headquarters have been preserved in a waterfront park along Will's Creek in Cumberland, Maryland. *Author's collection.*

Fort Necessity National Battlefield
1 Washington Parkway | Farmington, PA 15437
724-329-5512 | www.nps.gov/forne
GPS: 39.815527, -79.583025

The location of Washington's first battles, this historic site interprets several important French and Indian War events. Besides the fort, the park also preserves Jumonville Glen, the site of the first skirmish of the war; sections of Braddock's Road; and Braddock's grave. Looking out from the small fort to the open meadow, one can appreciate Washington's desperate situation here. The park also includes Washington Inn, a National Road–era tavern that links the area's early history to the later settlement and development of the region.

Frostburg Museum
PO Box 92
50 East Main Street | Frostburg, MD 21532
301-689-1195 | www.frostburgmuseum.org
GPS: 39.656898, -78.927138

This small museum explores local history, including the campaigns of Washington and Braddock.

Great Allegheny Passage
www.gaptrail.org

This 150-mile-long multiuse trail, an old railroad line, links Cumberland to Pittsburgh and incudes many sites related to the French and Indian War. The trail can be hiked or biked, and small segments can be visited. The best way to plan a trip here is to visit the website to determine where you want to access the trail.

Grantsville Community Museum
PO Box 413
153 Main Street | Grantsville, MD 2153
301-895-5454 | www.grantsvillemuseum.org/home
GPS: 39.696885, -79.155904

This museum has exhibits on local history, including the French and Indian War events that occurred in the area. Grantsville's Main Street lies on the site of the old Nemacolin Trail used by Washington and, later, Braddock.

Great Crossings Site
140 Marina Drive | Addison, PA 15411
GPS: 39.750326, -79.392994

In the 1940s, the Youghiogheny River was dammed as part of a flood control project, inundating the site of the Great Crossings. The ford was located south of the modern US-40 bridge, near Braddock Run. Today, the site can be viewed from the marina parking lot at Yough Lake. In the fall and winter, when the water level is low, the lake recedes to about the level of the old river, giving visitors a glimpse of what the crossing would have looked like in Washington's time. There are no facilities at the site.

The Great Crossings site. The Youghiogheny River was inundated and dammed as part of a flood control project in the 1940s. *Author's collection.*

Half King's Rock and Washington's Spring

Half King's Rock was the site of Tanacharison's camp before the Battle of Jumonville Glen. Here, Washington's Virginians met the Natives and began their march to attack. The site is visible from the road but is located on private property. Several historic markers are located near the site, though they are on a narrow road. Use caution when looking for these markers. One of these markers is also at the site of Washington's Spring.

Braddock Road Marker
GPS: 39 50.994, -79 39.448

This marker is at the intersection of National Pike (U.S. 40) and Jumonville Road (County Route 2021).

Washington-Braddock Road Rock Fort Camp Marker
GPS: 39 51.545, -79 38.709

This marker is on Jumonville Road (County Route 2021), one mile north of National Pike (U.S. 40).

Washington-Braddock Road Maker
GPS: 39 51.626, -79 38.659

This marker is on Jumonville Road (County Route 2021), 1.2 miles north of National Pike (U.S. 40).

Ohiopyle State Park
124 Main Street | Ohiopyle, PA 15470
www.dcnr.pa.gov/StateParks/FindAPark/OhiopyleStatePark/Pages/default.aspx
GPS: 39.86813, -79.4943

One of Pennsylvania's largest state parks includes thousands of wooded acres, waterfalls, hiking trails and more. This is where Washington encountered waterfalls in his attempt to find an all-water route to the Forks of the Ohio River. An outdoor exhibit tells visitors about Washington's journey, as do exhibits in the visitor center. The unspoiled landscape preserves the environment that the armies would have encountered in the 1750s. Thomas Faucet's grave is also found here; he was the soldier who allegedly shot General Braddock.

WASHINGTON'S SPRING
GPS: 39 51.628, -79 38.653

George Washington first stopped here in November 1753 on his mission to visit the French. He stopped here again in May 1754 and once again on the night of June 26, 1755, as part of Braddock's army. Washington himself did not name the spring, but local lore has attached his name to the landmark. A small spring does still flow here, down below the road. This marker is on Jumonville Road (Pennsylvania Route 2021), 1.2 miles north of National Pike (U.S. 40). There are no facilities at this site.

This marker notes the site of Washington Spring. Whether he stopped here the night of the march to Jumonville Glen is doubtful. *Author's collection.*

5

BRADDOCK

We will know better how to deal with them another time.
—General Edward Braddock's dying quote

In the spring of 1755, Pierre de Rigaud, Marquis de Vaudreuil, took the helm as governor in Quebec; he was New France's only Canadien-born governor-general. He inherited a colony on the brink of war.[1]

As the British escalated their efforts to retake the Ohio Country, Dinwiddie continued his appeals to leaders in London, noting that the French had invaded the territory of His Majesty the king. In the meantime, British authorities sent General Edward Braddock and two regiments of regular troops to assist Dinwiddie. It was a massive investment in the American colonies and part of a larger plan, the scale of which had not been undertaken before.

After taking Fort Duquesne, Braddock was to continue on to Niagara and cooperate with forces from New York and Massachusetts that were to attack the French forts at Crown Point and Niagara. It was overly ambitious and did not take into consideration the distances and logistical challenges of marching across North America.

Braddock today has a reputation of being uncreative, hardheaded, obstinate and arrogant. Perhaps these things are true, but his troops did not have time to train for wilderness warfare, and massive logistical challenges plagued the effort from start to finish. At sixty years old, Edward Braddock was a major general and the son of a major general. His father served in

Major General Edward Braddock was, strangely enough, the son of a major general. A career soldier, he served throughout Europe and commanded the garrison of Gibraltar before being summoned to North America. Braddock, however, lacked real combat experience and, of course, had no knowledge of the conditions on the American frontier. *New York Public Library.*

the Coldstream Guards, as he later would. The younger Edward Braddock was an ensign in the Coldstream Guards at age sixteen and later rose to the rank of lieutenant in the Guards Grenadier Company. He served in Holland in the 1740s but had limited combat experience. He then took the helm as the commander of the garrison at Gibraltar. Braddock had very little field experience and none while in command of a force this size.[2]

The two units sent under Braddock, the Forty-Fourth and Forty-Eighth Regiments, were peacetime garrison troops from Ireland. At about 660 men each, they were well under strength, though some men had combat experience from the Scottish Jacobite Rebellion of 1745. Sir Peter Halkett was the colonel commanding the Forty-Fourth Regiment, whose regimental facings were yellow. British infantry regiments wore red coats with different colors on the trim. The second-in-command of the Forty-Fourth was Lieutenant Colonel Thomas Gage. Colonel Thomas Dunbar led the Forty-Eighth Regiment, whose uniforms had buff trim. Lieutenant Colonel Ralph Burton was Dunbar's second-in-command.[3]

General Braddock is not usually associated with Virginia, but it was in the Old Dominion that he first set foot in North America, and it was there that he had his first taste of colonial diplomacy and began to address his numerous logistical challenges. Braddock's legacy is preserved by the modern road that winds through the modern suburbia of northern Virginia, though in many places, it does not follow the original route.

In March 1755, Braddock's forces arrived at Alexandria, and there, the two regular regiments were recruited up to full strength of 750 men each. But these were men of dubious quality and commitment. There was also precious little time for training of any kind, aside from learning the rudimentary handling of their muskets.[4]

Joining the expedition would be troops from the various colonies, including New York, Virginia, Maryland, North Carolina and South Carolina. Yet there was hardly a spirit of cooperation among them, and issues of supply and support plagued the effort and frustrated Braddock, who was accustomed to the relatively smooth and seamless work of the British military.[5]

Camp followers now have a bad reputation but were an important part of an eighteenth-century army. These ladies were part of the army; they were paid, they marched, they received rations, they suffered from the elements, they were subject to military discipline and, sometimes, they found themselves in combat. They were the wives of soldiers, and they often had children with them.

Camp followers performed essential support services and functions for armies that did not have large infrastructures or logistical support services. Camp followers primarily did the laundry and nursed the wounded. They also performed odd jobs, like herding cattle, sewing, gathering firewood, et cetera. No doubt, a bond formed among these women, who were a minority in a very male-dominated environment.

This could present a problem to an army if the women were not managed carefully. The British had developed a series of policies regulating the presence of women. A soldier had to have his officer's permission to marry, and the officer was to ensure that the woman he married was of good moral character and industrious. Regulations stated that an officer had to make a "strict inquiry…into the morals of the Woman." He was to determine "whether she is sufficiently known to be industrious, and able to earn her bread." The wives of soldiers were expected to be "honest, laborious Women."[6]

Many officers, like Braddock—and Washington later in the Revolution—felt that large numbers of women made the army look unprofessional and undermined discipline. While at Fort Cumberland, Braddock allowed six women per company in the British regiment and four per company among the Maryland and Virginia troops.

In mid-April, Braddock met with Dinwiddie and four other colonial governors at the John Carlyle House in Alexandria. The meeting was a high-profile affair and included an overview of all British strategy, not just Braddock's expedition to the Ohio Country. Braddock also brought up the touchy issues of funding and raising troops. The governors could not provide funding but agreed to marshal supplies and approach their legislatures for money. It was a sign of things to come. John Carlyle wrote to his brother George that "there was the Grandest Congress held at my home ever known on the Continent."[7]

As the army prepared to move out, it was plagued by issues of supply: a lack of wagons, difficulty in procuring food and issues with how to pay for it all. Due to the lack of wagons and horses available in Virginia, Sir Peter Halkett and the Forty-Fourth marched west from Alexandria, toward the mountains, while Colonel Thomas Dunbar, with Braddock himself and the Forty-Eighth, moved into Maryland and headed west. Bradxdock and the Forty-Eighth passed through the future site of Sharpsburg, where the Battle of Antietam later raged during the Civil War. The general and his staff passed along what is now Main Street.[8]

It was in Frederick, Maryland, that Deputy Postmaster for the Colonies Benjamin Franklin met with Braddock to arrange for mail delivery for the expedition. There, Franklin learned of Braddock's challenges with wagons and reached out to Pennsylvania's German communities to supply wagons for the army.[9]

At Fort Duquesne, spring flooding inundated the outer defense of the fort, necessitating repairs. Claude Pierre de Pècaudy Contrecoeur, the garrison

General Braddock met with several colonial governors at the Carlyle House in Alexandria, Virginia. It was one of the first times that a British officer met with colonial governors to coordinate a military effort. *New York Public Library.*

commander, hoped that reinforcements would arrive from Canada before Braddock did. Fort Duquesne dangled at the end of a long and tenuous supply line stretching back through portages and over water to Montreal, over seven hundred miles away.

In the meantime, Braddock's forces began arriving at Fort Cumberland, which overlooked Wills Creek, on May 10. On May 12 and 18, the general held councils with the Natives here. There were about forty Natives camped around the fort, along with some sixty women.[10]

The Natives included Delaware and Shawnee with Ohio Iroquois. The group included the Oneida Scaroyady (called Monacatootha by the Lenape, as he was a Half King), White Thunder and Silver Heels. A large contingent of Catawba were expected from the Carolinas but did not materialize.

Braddock was disappointed in the Native turnout but lacked the knowledge and skill to conduct effective frontier diplomacy, though Sir William Johnson (an experience diplomat) tried to assist. In his conferences with the Natives, Braddock showed respect and promised to restore their lands to them and to right previous wrongs. Only twenty-four Natives joined the march, and only eight accompanied the army the entire way. It was one of the greatest failures of the expedition.

Later accounts, possibly influenced by French propaganda or British officers with reputations to protect, describe Braddock as arrogant and uncooperative with the Natives. He was disappointed with the low turnout, but his actions were genuine and did not sabotage English relations with the Natives. The spring of 1755 was a low point for British prestige in the region, with the French in ascendance and gaining momentum from the previous year. The distrust between Braddock and Native leaders became mutual during the march, and later historians and writers have downplayed Braddock's efforts to recruit and retain Native allies before the campaign began.[11]

The army's march began on May 29; it was 125 miles to Fort Duquesne. Immediately, the going was tough, as the first mountain challenged the road builders west of the fort. Scouts found an alternate route that used the valley that passes through the mountain gap along Will's Creek called the Narrows.[12]

The army included many who would play roles later in American history: Lieutenant Colonel Thomas Gage (later commanded British forces in Boston at the start of the Revolution); waggoner Daniel Morgan (an American general during the Revolution who was known for the victory at Cowpens); another wagoner, Daniel Boone (later a frontiersman and

Markers in the streets and sidewalks note the bastions of Fort Cumberland, a unique way to mark the fort's location. *Author's collection.*

explorer who helped promote the Cumberland Gap); Captain Horatio Gates, who led a New York Independent Company and was wounded in the battle (later an American general at Saratoga and Camden); Captain Adam Stephen (commanded a division of American troops at Brandywine and Germantown); Lieutenant Charles Lee of the Forty-Fourth (an American General); and, of course, Washington.[13]

On the march, Braddock's army followed a strict routine: they were up by five o'clock most days, the guards moved ahead with the day's work detail and road construction began. The army moved ahead to the next campsite, and by evening, guards were posted around the perimeter.

The army moved in detachments. First were the guides, engineers and the Virginia Light Horse under Captain Robert Stewart, scouting ahead. Behind them was the advanced party of grenadiers and regulars who protected the working party. American provincials composed the working party building the road. Royal Navy sailors helped with block and tackle to move the guns over rough roads and steep ascents and descents. Off to the sides, parallel with the advanced guard, were flankers who were to prevent ambush. Behind this advanced guard was the main force of soldiers, followed by wagons and artillery, followed by a rear guard.[14]

Through June, as the British advanced and built their road, French and Native scouts spied on the column and occasionally sniped at the pickets. Yet Braddock's force was too large to engage directly, and the French and Natives hoped only to delay it. Back at Fort Duquesne, Contrecoeur pondered what to do. Scouts and spies watched and reported on the steady British progress and occasionally struck isolated British troops. If they made it to Fort Duquesne, Braddock's superior artillery would shell the fort into submission.

During this time, Washington had his most important impact on the campaign. He was serving as a volunteer aide-de-camp on Braddock's staff, avoiding the touchy issue of rank for a provincial officer. Based on intelligence that the French were getting reinforcements from Canada, the Virginia aide suggested that the army split up. Braddock, with the bulk of the infantry and some artillery, would move ahead to quickly take Fort Duquesne. The heavy wagons, baggage and most of the artillery, with a smaller force, would follow at its own pace, catching up when it could. Braddock adopted the plan and moved ahead with Halkett and the majority of the army's infantry. Colonel Dunbar, with the baggage and wagons, followed but was to never be more than a two days' march away.[15]

The majority of the healthy horses went with the flying column, as it was called, leaving Dunbar with the worn-out animals to haul wagons up the slope of Chestnut Ridge. Soon, the emaciated horses had to work in shifts, hauling wagons to the next camp, unhitching and returning to get the rest. Dunbar had advanced only a few miles beyond Great Meadows, near Jumonville Glen, when the flying column closed in on Fort Duquesne.[16]

The army spent the summer solstice, June 20, at a site called Bear Camp, just below the future Mason-Dixon line. Here, Washington, weak with illness, remained behind, hoping to catch up before the army took Fort Duquesne.[17]

On June 24, the army forded the Youghiogheny River at the Great Crossings after "a great deal of cutting and digging, and a few bridges." There were also brushes with French and Native scouts on the army's periphery. The ford itself was about one hundred yards wide and three feet deep. Today, the site lies under the Youghiogheny Lake, visible in the winter, when the water is drained and the lake resembles the river it used to be.[18]

Great Crossings was a local landmark for decades. In the 1810s, as the National Road was being constructed, largely paralleling Braddock's and Burd's Roads, the town of Somerfield grew at the site. In 1818, a three-arch stone bridge was dedicated by President James Monroe, with War of 1812

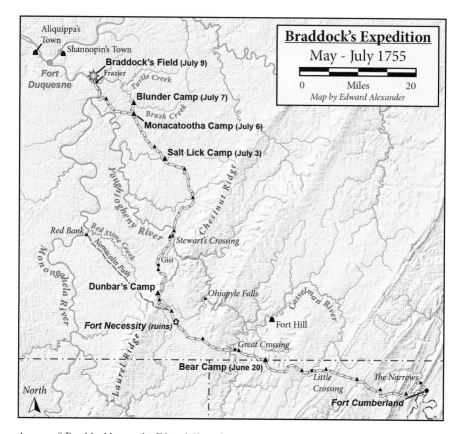

A map of Braddock's march. *Edward Alexander.*

veterans on hand. In 1944, the site was inundated as part of a flood control project, creating Lake Yough.

By the time the army arrived at the Great Meadows, it was clear their progress was far too slow. The charred ruins of Fort Necessity stood amid the shallow trenches and spiked, rusted swivel guns scattered about. One British officer noted, "There are many human bones round ye spot." The scene was a gloomy reminder of the cost of failure.[19]

On the afternoon of June 26, on Chestnut Ridge, above Jumonville Glen, British scouts found campfires burning and threats carved into the trees. Frenchmen and Natives lurking beyond the British scouts also fired on them before quickly withdrawing into the woods.[20]

After this incident and after the army crossed the Youghiogheny River at Stewart's Crossing, there were no more clashes from June 27 to July 5, as if the army seemed unstoppable to the French and Natives and they were unwilling to approach it again. North of the Youghiogheny River, the army moved through flatter terrain interspersed with meadows and swamps. Their progress was steady.[21]

One of the most experienced members of the expedition was absent for much of the march. George Washington's illness had gotten worse: burning fevers and aching pains, which debilitated him for most of June. He rejoined the army in early July, with General Braddock promising that he would be present for the capture of Fort Duquesne.[22]

July 2 found the army's provisions running low, and daily rations for the men were reduced to three-quarters of a pound of flour and half a pound of bacon. Braddock also sent for Washington, who arrived with a supply convoy.[23]

At Salt Lick Camp, named for the natural formation that drew animals to the site, Braddock held a council of war to discuss the army's plan going forward. The debate was over whether they should wait for Dunbar's column to catch up or push on to take Fort Duquesne without him. It was decided they should move ahead and take the fort, since waiting for Dunbar would take many days, and it was known that reinforcements were on the way to the Forks from Montreal.[24]

Near the modern town of Rillton on the night of July 6, the army established Monacatootha Camp about twenty miles from the Point. The campsite was named for what Sir Peter Halkett called an "unhappy incident." A few stragglers were killed by Natives beyond the army's perimeter, and a force of Grenadiers and friendly Natives set out to investigate. Friendly fire resulted in Scaroyady's (Monacatootha's) son being killed. Braddock ordered he be given a military funeral, and he bestowed gifts on Scaroyady. But it can only be imagined the impact the incident had on Scaroyady and the remaining Natives with the army.[25]

That same day, enemy Natives also killed a woman and a soldier on the army's fringe. Yet at Fort Duquesne, the mood was also melancholy. French and Native scouts reported that the army was getting closer every day and that it was so large, it seemed impossible to engage Braddock directly.[26]

The next day, the British army continued north along the Native path it had been following but turned off in an attempt to avoid the steep defiles of Turtle Creek, a perfect spot for an ambush. Yet the guides were either misled or missed their mark, for when the army arrived at Brush Creek, a steep defile confronted them; it was impossible to pass. This forced the army to retrace its steps and move west, toward the Monongahela River. That night, the men named their resting stop Blunder Camp.[27]

The army now had to cross the Monongahela River twice, which required a great deal of effort from the workmen, as they had to grade the riverbanks for the wagons and artillery. This route avoided the treacherous terrain of Turtle Creek, but fording a river (twice) had its own challenges with the extra work and the danger of facing an ambush at the vulnerable crossings.

On the morning of July 9, the members of the advanced party and the work crews were up by two o'clock. The first fording went smoothly, and the entire army eventually forded the river, marched up the west bank and recrossed near the mouth of Turtle Creek. Washington had been here before, as just above the creek sat John Frazier's cabin. The Virginian had just rejoined the army and had not quite recovered from his illness, but he was well enough to come and anxious to be present when the army took Fort Duquesne.[28]

By noon, the main army was crossing at the second ford. It was a sight to see: flags flying, fife and drums playing and troops confidently believing that the Point lay only eight miles away. Washington remembered the spectacle for the rest of his life.[29]

At Fort Duquesne, the tension was building, as Braddock's massive army was known to be closing in. By now, the Natives were unwilling to scout far from the fort, and Contrecoeur could get no good intelligence about Braddock's approach. The garrison commander was preparing to destroy the fort, seeing no alternative in the face of such overwhelming firepower. Captain Daniel Hyacinthe Lienard de Beaujeu, a forty-four-year-old officer, proposed intercepting Braddock's army at the second crossing of the river, and Contrecoeur agreed to try.[30]

The Natives camped around the Point outside of Fort Duquesne's walls included a variety of peoples from the region, as well as the Great Lakes and Canada. Among the hundreds of natives were Ottawas, Pottawatomies, Mississaugas, Kahnawakes, Winnebagos, Wyandots, Leni Lenapes, Ojibwas, Chippewas, Hurons, Iroquois (primarily Senecas), Sac, Fox, Miamis, Nipissings and Abenakis. It was the largest Native coalition yet assembled in North America.[31]

The Shawnee and Haudenosaunee readily agreed to attack alongside Beaujeu's soldiers, but the others were not so sure. The rumor was that the British had several thousand men and a large amount of artillery. It was an imposing force. On the night of July 8, Beaujeu met with the reluctant Natives outside the fort. They refused to go until Beaujeau gave an impassioned speech assuring them the English were weak and that he was confident of victory. Some were already wavering, and Beaujeu's words were enough to convince the rest.[32]

Captain Daniel Beaujeau inspired the reluctant Native allies to accompany the French to contest Braddock's army. He was killed in one of the first British volleys. *L'Historie des Canadiens-Francais.*

Thomas Gage commanded the advanced party of Braddock's army when it ran into the advancing French and Natives. Later, Gage commanded British troops in Boston at the start of the Revolution. *New York Public Library.*

Just after nine o'clock the next morning, July 9, the forces departed for the upper ford of the Monongahela River. Here, they hoped to ambush the British as they crossed, when they would be the most vulnerable. Prior to departing, Beaujeu prayed in the fort's small chapel.[33]

About 891 in total filed out, including troupes des marines, cadets, Canadien milice (totaling about 250 French) and 600 to 700 Natives from various nations. Just when the French were ready to give up without a fight, the momentum suddenly shifted, and the results were more than they could have hoped for.[34]

The Natives who marched off with the French were painted with a variety of colors and designs. Common body paint colors were black and red, made from bloodroot, red ocher and vermillion. Brown, blue and yellow, made from ocher, were also common colors.[35]

Beaujeu learned from scouts that the English had crossed the river and were approaching in a column. He had his force divided into three columns: two groups of Natives on either side with a French officer who spoke their language, and he personally led the middle column of French.[36]

Back at the second ford, as the main army was crossing, Lieutenant Colonel Gage led the advance party of about three hundred regulars and two six-pound guns ahead of the road-cutters. The ground sloped up and flattened. A long ridge to the right paralleled the river. The army was most vulnerable at the crossing, and with that obstacle behind them, the officers and men were confident they would take the French fort that afternoon or the next day.

As Gage's advanced party worked their way forward through the open woods; the guides ahead spotted a man stripped to the waist, directing a group behind him. It was Beaujeu. Gage formed his troops and fired a volley—then another. The French commander fell. The two six-pound guns with the advanced party fired about eighty rounds, crashing through the woods and tearing apart limbs and branches. It likely killed few Frenchmen or Natives, but it was terrifying.[37]

The Natives spread to the right and left, surrounding Gage's force and firing on it, while the French remained in the center. With casualties mounting, Gage directed his small force back. Hearing the firing, a relief force came rushing up and crashed into Gage's retiring troops. The confused mass was then hit by the incoming fire from all sides.[38]

Canadien soldier Jolicoeur Charles Bonin wrote:

> *Immediately the order was given to advance in double-quick time, and to attack the enemy simultaneously from the front and both flanks. This order was hastily carried out. The savages shouted their war cry, and the French opened fire with a volley, which was followed by a volley from the savages. The enemy, taken by surprise, formed a line of battle, and fired their artillery. De Beaujeu was killed by the first volley; and the savages, terrified by the unfamiliar noise of the cannon, took flight momentarily. But Captain Dumas took command immediately after Sieur de Beaujeu's death and encouraged the French. The savages saw the steadfastness of the Frenchmen and no longer heard the cannon, which the French had seized. They, therefore, returned to charge the enemy, following the French example, and forced them to retreat.[39]*

Captain Jean Daniel Dumas, the second-in-command, provided inspired leadership after Beaujeu's death. It was a tense moment, and it could have gone either way. Dumas was forty-three years old in 1755. He later served as the mayor of Quebec, and after the war, he was governor of Mauritius in the Indian Ocean and retired as a major general of the army. He died in 1794, having seen much of the world and a great many changes in his lifetime.[40]

Dumas reported, "It was then, that by word and gesture I sought to rally the few soldiers who remained. I advanced, with an assurance born of despair." A common misconception is that the French and Natives ambushed Braddock, when in fact, the two sides bumped into each other. Having come up short of their goal of meeting the British at the second crossing was bad enough for the French, but within the first few minutes, they lost their commander, the inspiring Beaujeu. It was a worst-case scenario, and at that crucial moment, things could have gone either way, yet the French rallied and struck back (though it is more properly a Native victory). It is another reminder that the overwhelming victory was a near-run thing.[41]

The British troops deployed and began firing toward the unseen enemy. The land sloped steeply to the river, making battle lines and advance difficult. The woods were open, proving good cover for the enemy. Most never saw their attackers, except for the occasional shadow darting from tree to tree in the distance or the flashes of muzzles.

The men of the two regiments became crowded together, creating confusion and offering a target in which many men could be wounded or killed by one incoming shot. Soon, the artillerymen were driven from their guns or incapacitated. Virginia troops turned off to the north, taking cover in the woods; many used a massive fallen log for shelter. Unfortunately, the British troops behind them fired into them by mistake.[42]

Washington emerged as a hero of the battle, having had his hat and coat shot through. He rallied the troops in the aftermath and spoke highly of the Virginians who fought well in the woods. Washington wrote, "The Virginia Companies Behaved like Men, and died like Soldiers."[43]

Christopher Gist saw a Native take aim at Sir Peter Halkett, who was commanding the Forty-Fourth Regiment but was unable to reload his weapon fast enough; the Native shot the colonel. Halkett's son, Lieutenant James Halkett, ran to assist him, but was also killed. Father and son lay together on the ground.[44]

Gage noted that "a visible Terror and Confusion appeared amongst the Men." Braddock attempted to rally the troops by various means. He had the color guards of the two regiments move to opposite areas so the men could see their unit's flag and regroup. He ordered the troops to fire by platoon, relying on the deadly volleys that were often effective in combat. He ordered the twelve-pound guns to move to the left of the road to fire in that direction. Nothing worked.[45]

The French and Natives were working their way around both flanks, firing into the mass of confused men. Eventually, they had the entire army surrounded on three sides. French accounts of the battle agree that the Natives acted on their own and instinctively. They took no orders from the French once the battle began and moved along, leapfrogging along the length of the British army. French officers familiar with the Native languages and customs accompanied each Native group.[46]

Braddock ordered Colonel Ralph Burton to lead some grenadiers and troops from the Forty-Fourth to take the commanding hill to their right,

The neighborhoods of Braddock and North Braddock from across the river. The battle began near the high rise on the left, and in the background is the large hill the Natives seized. *Author's collection.*

from which the enemy was pouring fire into them. This involved charging a quarter mile through wooded ground toward a crest they could not see due to the forest. These attacks failed to dislodge the French and Natives there. Braddock criticized any troops who broke ranks to fight behind the trees, insisting that they fight in linear formation. Although the Virginians were experienced with this mode of warfare, the British were not, and ordering the entire army to fight that way may have caused more confusion and casualties by friendly fire.[47]

Braddock rode everywhere and had four horses shot from under him. He was eventually hit, the ball going through his arm and into his lung. Washington and several others saw to it that he was taken off the field. After standing their ground for three hours, the army began to unravel, with more and more men breaking and running for the river. Braddock ordered a retreat all the way back to Dunbar's camp. The battlefield was littered with the dead and wounded, abandoned wagons and equipment and the bodies of at least eight of the British army's camp followers.[48]

The column, with many walking wounded, struggled south along the road they had cut, passing old campsites and landmarks. Wagon drivers who had cut their horses loose arrived at Dunbar's camp the next day with word of the disaster, but the main column of survivors limped in on July 11. Braddock ordered barrels of flour to be left along the road for stragglers, and many noted this helped them survive the retreat. The army had taken days to march the fifty-seven miles from Dunbar's camp to the Monongahela River, but they made it all the way back in just two days. Having marched, fought a battle and retreated, the men were physically exhausted.[49]

Bonin described the incredible haul in the aftermath: baggage wagons, ten cannons (spiked and left on the field), three mortars, fifteen flags and hundreds of weapons. He was detailed to stay on the battlefield overnight guarding the equipment until it could all be removed later. Bonin did not relish sleeping among the dead and wounded, and nearly became a casualty himself when he feared that a drunk Native near him would turn on him in his stupor.

Eleven Frenchmen were killed and twenty-two were wounded, while two Natives were killed and twenty were wounded. In total, the French/Native forces had thirteen killed and forty-two wounded in the lopsided victory. Contrecoeur noted that "such a victory was entirely unexpected."[50]

Back at Fort Duquesne, an English prisoner named James Smith had watched the attack force sally out to meet Braddock. Smith hoped that his liberation was at hand, but his spirit sank when, later that afternoon, he saw Natives returning, loaded with loot and with prisoners in tow. That evening, English soldiers who were taken in the battle were tortured and burned to death along the banks of the Allegheny River.[51]

The French brought Beaujeu's body back to Fort Duquesne, where it was put on display for mourning and then buried there days later. The location of the garrison cemetery has long been lost, as it was destroyed in the intervening two hundred years of floods and development of the city. Somewhere near the Point lie the remains of the architect of this victory and other French soldiers. The register of baptisms and burials from Forts Duquesne, Machault, Le Bouef and Presque Isle survive in Montreal, providing details of the deaths and burials at the fort.[52]

Braddock's exhausted and melancholy force began retreating back to Fort Cumberland, abandoning supplies like weapons and ammunition at Dunbar's camp. Powder was dumped, shells were tossed into the woods and other material was damaged and abandoned.

The general died on the march, around eight o'clock on Sunday evening, July 13. The defeat weighed heavily on his mind as he uttered, "Who would have thought it?" Among his last words were, "We will know better how to deal with them another time."[53]

His body was buried in the road itself, and the army marched over the site to obliterate it and hide the body from the depredations of the Natives.

General Braddock's body remained hidden until 1804, when workers who were repairing the road found the grave. Colonel Thomas Dunbar took command of the surviving forces as the senior officer remaining. Rumors of the disaster began reaching Fort Cumberland, where British army nurse Charlotte Brown was stationed. She noted that soldiers' wives who were left behind were anxious and worried. Confirmation came soon enough.

From Fort Cumberland, Dunbar left with the troops on August 2 for Philadelphia, essentially abandoning the frontier to its fate. The effects of Braddock's defeat were swift and brutal. Using Braddock's Road in reverse, French and Native troops raided the frontier from Pennsylvania to southern Virginia with impunity that summer. Settlers banded together in private homes and forts. Militia patrols attempted to interdict the raiders, yet it seemed nothing could stop the violence.[54]

Braddock's Field, as it was called, became a local landmark in the nineteenth century. The unburied dead lay on the ground, and visitors noted the skulls and bones. As the field was located near the growing town of Pittsburgh, settlers gradually cleared the land, but it remained mostly undeveloped until the Civil War. The site was a rallying point in 1794, during the Whiskey Rebellion, and in 1804, Judge George Wallace, the first president judge of the court of Allegheny County, built a mansion here. Lafayette visited the site on his American tour in 1825.[55]

In the late 1800s, the towns of Braddock and North Braddock rose on the site of the battle. Their development brought grading for homes and roads and the construction of basements, underground utility lines and other disturbances, yet the general lay of the land remains intact. In 1873, Andrew Carnegie constructed the massive Edgar Thomson steel mill along the river, obscuring the crossing site and the location of Frazier's cabin. Turtle Creek was even rerouted to make way for the enormous mill. The massive plant, the last operating steel mill in the region, towers over the neighborhood. Perhaps it is fitting that this iconic symbol of the region's industry is tied to the battlefield and one of the most important historic events that occurred in the area.

The battle was a watershed event at the time, and it has resonated through American history as one of the worst military defeats at the hands of Native, ranking with Little Bighorn and St. Clair's defeat. It also stands out among the defeats in British military history along with Isandlwana (the Anglo-Zulu War, 1879) and the Somme (World War I, 1916).

The British army lost 60 percent of its force at the Monongahela, an unheard-of statistic. Furthermore, the rate of killed to wounded was much

Road workers discovered Braddock's remains in 1804 and moved them to a nearby hilltop. Wooden markers noted the site for one hundred years until local preservation groups placed this monument here in 1913. *Author's collection.*

higher than was typical for conflicts of this period, with over 50 percent of the casualties being killed as opposed to a more typical 25 percent.[56]

Ironically, the terrible and important battle has not one but many commonly accepted names: Braddock's Defeat, the Battle of Braddock's Field, the Battle of the Monongahela and the Battle of Turtle Creek. The Native participants had never seen anything like it. At a small cost, they had destroyed a larger British army. After they returned to villages along the Great Lakes, the St. Lawrence and Ohio Rivers and others, word spread of the great victory and the prowess of the Native warriors.

Perhaps the most lingering controversy from the campaign and this battle is Braddock himself. He has been both vilified and defended by participants and later historians. The general clearly made mistakes; he obviously had little experience in direct command of an army. Despite his unprecedented challenges in supply, logistics and training, Braddock succeeded in advancing British forces hundreds of miles into the interior of North America for the first time and forever breached the Appalachian Mountain barrier with his road.

Braddock was described by contemporaries as arrogant and stubborn, but he was also loyal and determined. Benjamin Franklin wrote of him following the defeat: "This general was, I think, a brave man and might probably have made a figure as a good officer in some European war. But he had too much self confidence, too high an opinion of the validity of regular troops, and too mean a one of both American and Indians."

Washington noted that Braddock was "a man whose good and bad qualities were intimately blended. He was brave even to a fault and in regular Service would have done honor to his profession." The campaign and Braddock himself had lasting impacts on Washington, who later wore the general's sash and pistols in the Revolution. They are now on display at Mount Vernon.[57]

As the weather cooled and the leaves turned vibrant colors in the fall of 1755, Captain Dumas could look out with satisfaction at the mighty rivers flowing past Fort Duquesne. These waters drained half a continent, flowing down to the French post at New Orleans. The Forks of the Ohio River and the lands they drained were securely in French hands.

Sites to Explore

Braddock's Battlefield History Center
609 Sixth Street | Braddock, PA 15104
WWW.BRADDOCKSBATTLEFIELD.COM
GPS: 40 40.5574, -79 86.4293

Until 2012, there was no history museum dedicated to one of the largest battles of the entire colonial period. Today, the museum features exhibits with many artifacts from the battlefield and campsites, and it hosts special events. The museum sits at the site of the battle's start in a suburb of Pittsburgh.

Braddock's Grave
(Part of Fort Necessity National Battlefield)
Route 40, West of Farmington, PA
WWW.NPS.GOV/FONE/BRADDOCKGRAVE
GPS: 39 49.945, -79 36.069

Here, in the middle of the road, Braddock's officers buried the dead general to hide his body. Then the army marched over the site to obliterate it. In

THIS TABLET MARKS THE SPOT WHERE
MAJOR-GENERAL EDWARD BRADDOCK WAS
BURIED, JULY 14th, 1755.
HIS REMAINS WERE REMOVED IN 1804
TO THE SITE OF THE PRESENT MONUMENT.

Braddock's original grave site is a short walk down the old roadbed from the parking lot of the roadside park. Here, the general was buried, and the army marched over the site to obliterate its trace. *Author's collection.*

1804, some workmen discovered human remains in the road near where Braddock was supposed to have been buried. An officer's uniform buttons were reportedly found at the site and indicated that the remains were those of General Braddock. Today, the grave site is marked just below a 1913 monument that stands over the general's final resting place.

BRADDOCK ROAD PRESERVATION ASSOCIATION
WWW.BRADDOCKROADPA.ORG

This group promotes the study of the road and historic sites along the route. It holds an annual conference with speakers and exhibits.

BRADDOCK ROAD TRACE NO. 1
GPS: 39 74.6, -79 44.7

Located off Route 40, near Markelysburg, Pennsylvania, this is a two-and-a-half-mile section of the original road that you can drive. Start at the intersection of Braddock Road and Route 281, and turn left onto Braddock Road. This stretch ends at Flat Road, where turning right will return you to Route 40. At the northern terminus, the old road continued straight ahead, but it is now a driveway and goes on into the woods beyond.

Braddock Road Trace No. 2
GPS: 39 85.0, -79 65.7

Beginning at the summit of Laurel Ridge, this six-mile section is drivable and passes by landmarks such as Half King's Rock, Washington's Spring, Jumonville Glen, Honeycomb Rock and Dunbar's Camp.

Begin at the intersection of Route 40 and Jumonville Road, across from the Summit Inn. You will pass by the site of Half King Rock on your left (inaccessible) and Washington's Spring on your right (marked but also, as of this writing, inaccessible). The road joined the modern road here from the right (east). From here on, the modern road follows the historic path. Washington's spring is just off the road, but it is marked as private property. Here, the officer and his men stopped on their way to Jumonville Glen. Farther on, you will pass Jumonville Glen, the site of the ambush, and farther yet is Honeycomb Rock, a massive boulder and local landmark where you can pull over. As you begin to descend the old road ran north and is not traceable. The modern road continues down to eventually join Route 119, where you can drive north to see the Meason House/Gist's Plantation site.

Braddock Rock
GPS: 38 89.2743, -77 05.1425

Local legend claims that Braddock stepped on a rocky ledge in what is now Washington, D.C., soon after arriving in Virginia. The landscape and shoreline have been altered over the years, and today, a remnant of the rock is preserved at the bottom of a well near the Theodore Roosevelt Bridge in Foggy Bottom. This site is located along the west side of Route 50 across from the Institute of Peace. There are no facilities at the site.

Braddock's Spring Marker
1300 Braddock Avenue | Braddock, PA 15104
GPS: 40 23.821, -79 51.571

According to legend, near here, the wounded general was treated at a spring and then removed from the battlefield as the army collapsed around him. The marker sits in front of the massive Edgar Thomson Steel Mill. There are no facilities at the site.

BRADDOCK STONE
44 EAST MAIN STREET | FROSTBURG, MD 21532
GPS: 39 39.418, -78 55.641

This colonial highway marker is named for Braddock and stood alongside the road in Frostburg, Maryland. It has been moved several times and was once even cut in half and put back together. The stone and several historic markers now stand in downtown Frostburg. There are no facilities at the site.

CARLYLE HOUSE
121 NORTH FAIRFAX STREET | ALEXANDRIA, VA 22314
703-549-2997
WWW.NOVAPARKS.COM/PARKS/CARLYLE-HOUSE-HISTORIC-PARK
GPS: 38 80.5226, -77 4.201

This imposing mansion, owned by merchant John Carlyle, was Braddock's headquarters when he arrived in Virginia. The house offers guided tours, and you can explore the outdoor gardens.

DUNBAR'S CAMP
GPS: 39 52.943, -79 38.778

Colonel Thomas Dunbar, with the bulk of the army's wagons and artillery, had advanced as far as this spot from Great Meadows when disaster struck the

Dunbar's camp is marked with signs and includes several walking trails. It was the scene of great panic after the survivors of Braddock's defeat arrived here. *Author's collection.*

advanced force. When the remnants of the army reached this site, Dunbar had their supplies destroyed and scattered into the woods. The army then retreated back down the road toward Fort Cumberland. Several historic markers stand here, and walking trails wind through the forest. This marker is located on Jumonville Road (Pennsylvania Route 2021), three miles north of National Pike (U.S. 40). There are no facilities at the site.

FORT CUMBERLAND AND WASHINGTON'S HEADQUARTERS
16 WASHINGTON STREET | CUMBERLAND, MD 21502
WWW.EMMANUELPARISHOFMD.ORG/FORT-CUMBERLAND
GPS: 39 65.0866, -78 76.5523

The fort was 400 by 120 feet and served as the logistical headquarters for the army under the command of General Braddock. It was the largest military installation in North America at that time. In the summer of 1755, about five thousand men, women and children resided here, making it one of the largest settlements on the frontier for a few months. Outlines on the ground and historic markers surrounding Emmanuel Church note the site of the fort. A self-guided walking tour takes visitors around the site of the fort and Washington's headquarters.

GREAT ALLEGHENY PASSAGE TRAIL
DUQUESNE PARKING AREA
20 LIBRARY PLACE | DUQUESNE, PA 15110

MCKEESPORT PARKING AREA
201 WATER STREET | MCKEESPORT, PA 15132

HOMESTEAD PARKING AREA | 191 EAST WATERFRONT DRIVE
HOMESTEAD, PA 15120

WWW.GAPTRAIL.ORG

A portion of this walking/biking has views of the fords of the Monongahela River and the battle site of July 9. An eight-mile stretch between McKeesport and Homestead takes you past the sites of the army's river crossing and the battle, and there are a few markers noting Braddock's Road, which actually hugged the river nearby. The McKeesport Connecting Bridge crosses the river at Braddock's first fording site. The trail also passes by Stewart's Ford at Connellsville.

Heinz History Center
1212 Smallman Street | Pittsburgh, PA 15222
www.heinzhistorycenter.org
GPS: 40 44.6849, -79 99.2077

This museum tells the story of Pittsburgh's history with a special emphasis on the French and Indian War.

Meason House/Gist's Plantation Site
At the End of Cellurale Drive, off Route 119 North
GPS: 39 57.14, -79 38.52

This is private property, but the house can be viewed from the driveway. The 1802 house sits on the site of Christopher Gist's plantation. The house is one of only two full Palladian-style homes (with all seven elements of Palladian architecture) still standing in the nation.

The Narrows
GPS: 39 39.776, -78 46.867

Three historic markers stand at this site along the old National Road, just north of Cumberland. You will have a spectacular view of the Narrows here. The markers and parking area are located just north of Cumberland on Alt. U.S. 40.

Braddock's army initially tried to build its road straight west from Fort Cumberland but found the going too tough. They settled on the gap called the Narrows, following Will's Creek. *Author's collection.*

Rindfuss Museum, Jumonville Conference Center
887 Jumonville Road | Hopwood, PA 15445
724-439-4912 | www.jumonville.org/history-british

An exhibit in Murphy Lodge has artifacts from Dunbar's camp as well as Braddock's march. Check ahead for information on hours and access.

Stewart's Crossing
Connellsville, PA 15425
GPS: 40 1.222, -79 36.047

Here, Braddock's army camped and then crossed the Youghiogheny River. A historic marker notes the crossing and sits astride the Great Allegheny Passage Trail. The marker is located in the Yough River Park, seventy-five yards west of the corner of North Seventh Street and Torrence Avenue. There are no facilities at the site.

Washington Monument, Braddock Battlefield
GPS: 40 24.178, -79 51.799

The only monument on the battlefield, it stands amid the modern town of Braddock, near the center of the scene of fighting. This marker is located on Jones Avenue, 0.1 miles south of Bell Avenue, in Braddock, Pennsylvania, 15104. There are no facilities at this site.

Washington is honored with a monument in the center of the battlefield on a city street. *Author's collection.*

THE FRONTIER IN FLAMES

Blood on the moon.
—Colonel James Inns

Following Braddock's defeat and Dunbar's withdrawal, the French and Natives struck with a vengeance on the vulnerable frontier. Virginia and Pennsylvania, two of the most prosperous British colonies, found themselves powerless to defend their citizens and unable to contribute anything meaningful to the war effort.

As a colony founded by Quaker William Penn and dominated in its assembly by Quakers, Pennsylvania was unique in that it was the only British colony without compulsory military service. It had no militia and no tradition of organizing troops and military planning, making it particularly vulnerable. There were plenty who saw this glaring defect and worked to correct it as the war unfolded.

On a Sunday morning in July 1755, a band of Shawnee Natives raided Draper Meadow near modern-day Blacksburg, Virginia. The attackers killed four settlers and took five hostages, including Mary Draper Ingles and two of her sons. Ingles was taken on a long journey into modern Kentucky and Ohio by the Shawnee.

When Mary found the chance to escape, she and another woman made their way back, crossing rivers and subsisting in the wilderness until they made it back to their home area. Forty-two days after setting out, Mary arrived at the home of a neighbor on December 1, and she was reunited

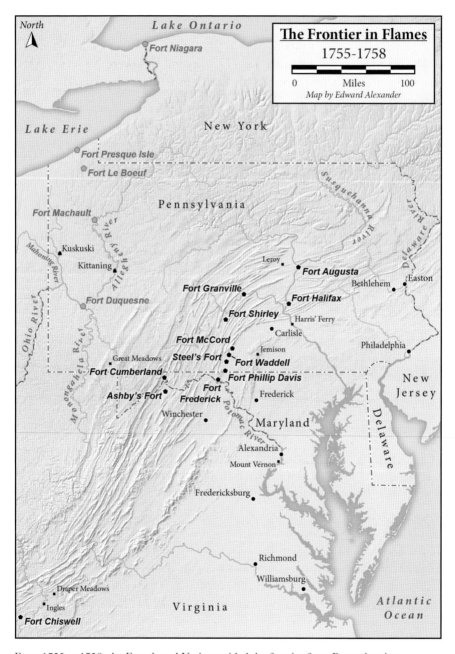

From 1755 to 1758, the French and Natives raided the frontier from Pennsylvania to Virginia. *Edward Alexander.*

with her husband. She is honored at several sites in southwestern Virginia and on Richmond's Capitol Square in the Virginia Women's Monument.

On the morning of October 16, 1775, several Delaware Natives entered Barbara Leninger's home on Penn's Creek in modern-day Union County, Pennsylvania, announcing, "We are Alleghany Indians and your enemies. You must all die." Over three days, the raiding party killed nineteen and took over ten prisoners. This raid has been remembered as the Penn's Creek Massacre. Natives attacked near Harris' Ferry (modern-day Harrisburg) that same month. Another group struck the Great Cove area near Chambersburg, and still others raided along Pennsylvania's Juniata River.[1]

A month later, on November 14, a French and Native force from Fort Duquesne struck settlements in Berks County, just fifty miles from Philadelphia. Ten days later, they attacked settlements in the Leigh Valley, only thirty miles from Bethlehem.[2]

One observer at Bethlehem noted, "Men, Women, and Children who had lately lived in great Affluence and Plenty reduced to the most extreme Poverty and Distress…and in want of the Common Necessaries of Life." Refugees fled east, leaving the frontier for the settled areas of the colony.[3]

Pennsylvania's frontier settlers demanded action. They needed protection from the raids, but help was not forthcoming from their government. The leadership was stalemated, as animosity between the Penns and Quakers in the assembly ran deep.

Governor Thomas Penn, the son of the colony's founder, William Penn, refused to pay any tax on the family's vast land holdings, and the Quakers repeatedly attempted to do so. The Penns also pushed for military defense, but the Quakers refused to authorize the funds for warfare. The two sides argued for years. In 1756, many Quakers were persuaded not to run for assembly seats, and slowly, their influence dwindled. But the assembly as a whole insisted on taxing the Penns' lands. By 1756, nothing had changed, and there matters stood, with no resolution in sight. In the meantime, the frontier burned.[4]

Philadelphia printer Benjamin Franklin had addressed the problem a decade earlier during King George's War in 1747. Franklin and his colleagues formed a private militia called the Associators. It was entirely voluntary and privately funded. The Associators re-formed in 1755 to meet the growing crisis, but they were not enough. What Pennsylvania needed was a real military.[5]

As the stalemate between Thomas Penn and the assembly dragged on over taxes and funding, families on the frontier demanded action. Finally

Mary Ingles Draper is represented in the Women's Memorial on Virginia's Capitol Square in Richmond. The monument highlights important women in the state's history. *Author's collection.*

on November 25, 1755, the colony approved a militia law sponsored by Benjamin Franklin. The militia was voluntary, so pacifists did not have to serve. And it had several key components to make it more appealing to Quakers, like the provision that a soldier would not spend more than three days away from home. It was designed for local defense and was overall a weak program, but it was a start.[6]

Raids on the frontier continued, and Pennsylvania's militia was not able to stop them. Recognizing the need for a true military force, Pennsylvania created a provincial regiment in 1756, and for the first time since the colony's founding in 1681, it had an official military force like the other colonies. Provincial troops were raised and equipped by each colony for defense and military operations. Their uniforms and equipment were similar to those of the British regulars.[7]

The breakthrough came from a compromise between Thomas Penn and the assembly. The pacifist-leaning assembly agreed to spend money for military defense as long as it was funded by a donation from Penn. The donation was equivalent to the taxes that would have been placed on his lands.[8]

In April 1756, Pennsylvania did the unthinkable: the colony declared war on the Delaware, including setting scalp bounties as incentives. The colony founded on the principle of peaceful relations with the Natives was now at war with them.

In the spring of 1756, Captain John Daniel Sieur Dumas, who had seized the initiative at the start of the battle with Braddock, took command of Fort Duquesne. Captain Contrecoeur was in poor health and had asked to be relieved and returned to his home near Quebec. He died in 1775 as American troops were closing in on Quebec during the Revolution. He was called by then-governor Guy Carlton "the third most influential Canadian."[9]

In December 1756, Colonel Francois-Marie Le Marchand de Ligneris relieved Captain Dumas at Fort Duquesne. Dumas returned to Quebec and later fought at the closing battles of the war in Quebec and Sainte Foy. Dumas eventually rose to the rank of general in the French army and died in France in 1794. His finest hour was on the banks of the Monongahela River.[10]

Over time, the French expanded Fort Duquesne at the Point, building a stockade out from the main fort. Beyond that were crops and gardens

The site of Fort Duquesne is outlined in Point State Park in Pittsburgh. *Author's collection.*

to augment the garrison's meager rations. Various Native groups camped nearby and across the Allegheny River to the north.

Louis-Joseph de Montcalm-Grozon, Marquis de Montcalm, the overall military commander in New France, knew of the fort's weaknesses despite having never seen the site. He wrote in 1756, "Fort Duquesne is not worth a straw. A freshet nearly carried it off a short time ago." Spring floods from melting snow inundated the fort, causing the garrison to make repairs to the stockade and earthworks. In fact, floods plagued the later city of Pittsburgh well into the twentieth century, often covering the entire downtown area. A flood control project in the 1940s alleviated the problem, but it also submerged the site of Great Crossings on the Youghiogheny River.[11]

War between France and England was officially declared on May 17, 1756. Maryland then took steps to protect its frontier with the construction of Fort Frederick between modern-day Hagerstown and Hancock. The fort was unusually strong, built of stone rather than wood.

By 1756, there were sixty-eight private forts in Virginia and about fifty in Pennsylvania. Settlers fortified their homes and, in some cases, built blockhouses. They served as bases from which local militia could gather and patrol between them and were points of shelter where neighboring families gathered in times of danger.[12]

In July 1756, a party from the Delaware village of Kittaning on the Allegheny River attacked and burned Fort Granville to the ground (at modern-day Lewistown, Pennsylvania). The leader of the French and Native force was Captain Coulon de Villiers, who had led the attack at Fort Necessity. The fall of this strongpoint showed the frontier's continued vulnerability.[13]

Through the summer of 1756, the Natives raided down the Shenandoah River in western Virginia and into Augusta, Bedford, Halifax and Lunenburg Counties. By this time, Pennsylvania fielded 1,400 troops, which was more than all the French forts in the Ohio Country combined held. The French strength from a French letter, was as follows:

	Officers	Cadets	Milice and Soldiers	Total
Fort Duquesne	6	15	237	258
Venango Camp	1	0	15	16
Fort Le Bouef	1	2	85	88
Fort Presque Isle	1	2	100	103

Total in the Ohio Country: 465[14]

During their raids, the French and Natives drove off livestock, destroyed crops, burned down homes and wreaked havoc on the inhabitants of the frontier. One typical French report noted:

> *All of the Nations of la Belle Riviere have taken up the hatchet against the English. The first party that was formed in that quarter, since the last report… was composed of two hundred and fifty Indians, to whom the Commandant at Fort Duquesne had joined some Frenchmen at the request of those Indians.*
>
> *This party divided themselves into small squads, at the height of land, and fell on the settlements beyond Fort Cumberland, defeated a detachment of twenty regulars.…After these different squads had destroyed or carried away several families, pillaged and burnt several houses, they came again together.…This party returned to Fort Duquesne with sixty prisoners and a great number of scalps.*[15]

A new British prime minister came to power in December 1756, and his leadership altered the course of the war. William Pitt implemented a new strategy, reducing British oversight, allowing Americans to have a greater role in the conflict and spending freely on the war. Money was no object, and Pitt had the British treasury cover the recruiting and supplying costs for provincial troops. Pitt was celebrated after the war for his role in defending the colonies and defeating the French. Most notably, he is honored by the city that bears his name.[16]

Pennsylvania was ready to take the war to the Natives by the fall of 1756. The target was the large Native village of Kittanning on the Allegheny River, only forty miles from Fort Duquesne. The village was an important Delaware town and a launching point for raids on the frontier. Chief Shingas and Tewa (also known as Captain Jacobs) resided here. Pennsylvania governor Robert Hunter Morris appointed Lieutenant Colonel John Armstrong to lead the expedition. John's brother was the commander who was killed at Fort Granville earlier in the summer.

Armstrong took three hundred men 122 miles from Fort Shirley (at modern-day Shirleysburg), closely following modern U.S. 22 and U.S. 422. On September 8, they struck in total surprise, killing forty, including Tewa. The Pennsylvanians also lost about forty. Wounded in the attack was Captain Hugh Mercer, who was shot in wrist. He made his way alone back to Fort Lyttleton and safety, avoiding Native patrols and surviving on berries. Mercer later commanded American troops in the Revolution and was killed at the Battle of Princeton.[17]

The raid showed that Pennsylvania was not powerless and could strike back, and it showed the weaknesses of the Lenape. Armstrong later served in the Forbes expedition, and afterward, he was a general in the Revolution, fighting at Brandywine and Germantown. He then served in the state assembly and Continental Congress.[18]

In the winter of 1756–57, the Natives raided into Berks and Northampton Counties, well within the settled area of Pennsylvania. Then in the spring of 1757, groups of Shawnee, Potawatomis and Ottawa attacked the Chambersburg area.[19]

Although they did not directly attack the fort, the Natives harassed the garrison at Fort Cumberland, Maryland, and attacked nearby settlements. Militia officer Adam Stephens wrote to Washington, "Nothing is to be seen or heard but Desolation and Murder….The Smoke of Burning plantations darken the day and hide the neighboring mountains." Colonel James Inns, the commander at Fort Cumberland, wrote that every night, there was "blood on the moon."[20]

From 1756 to 1757, Washington served as colonel of the Virginia Regiment, responsible for defending the colony's western frontier from Native attacks. The assignment was an impossible one, and in many ways, it prepared Washington for the challenges ahead. The young colonel had to defend a frontier covering over three hundred miles with less than one thousand men. His militia came and went; their pay was low, and supplies were difficult to procure. Letters for help were sent to the Virginia assembly in Williamsburg, but they were met with little success. Washington's defense fell apart as parties of French and Native raiders moved between forts and struck settlements.[21]

In June 1757, for example, Virginia instituted a draft, yet its provisions hindered Washington's ability to meet the enemy threats. His militia could not leave the colony, and the enlistments were short term. Desertions were rampant, and morale sank. Culpeper County's quota was one hundred men; eighty arrived, but only twenty-five were armed. Twenty men deserted out of a ninety-man detachment from Fredericksburg. At one point, over one hundred of four hundred men deserted at Winchester, leaving after they were paid and clothed. Washington could barely equip and train his men before either they deserted or their enlistments expired. His regiment became a revolving door.[22]

The years of border defense are probably the most overlooked of Washington's early military career, but they gave the rising officer invaluable experience dealing with militia, supplying his troops and working with an

Left: The raid on the Lenape village at Kittanning on the Allegheny River was the first major offensive action taken by Pennsylvania during the war. This marker recalls the attack. *Author's collection.*

Below: Washington's headquarters in Winchester is a museum, one of the few colonial-era structures surviving in the town. Washington oversaw frustrating attempts to guard Virginia's frontier from here. *Author's collection.*

elected assembly. In his Winchester headquarters, he learned how to manage a war effort—from raising troops to raising money.

At Fort Chiswell, which was built to protect Virginia's southwestern frontier, an incident occurred that reverberated years later. A twenty-year-old wagon driver irritated a British lieutenant, who struck the colonial man with his sword. In return, Daniel Morgan knocked out the officer with a single blow and was disciplined with a sentence of 500 lashes on the back. Later, Morgan served as a general in the Revolution and loved to tell the story of how the British miscounted and gave him only 499 lashes, saying they owed him one lash. Morgan commanded the American army in the victory at Cowpens, South Carolina.

By 1758, the larger tide of the war was turning against the French. British naval superiority began to cut off supplies from France to Canada. As trade goods dwindled, the French along La Bella Riviera could not meet the needs of their Native allies. Years of warfare had reduced the annual crop harvests in New France as well. Farm production was down, as men were serving in the Canadien milice. British reinforcements were arriving in New York and New England to bolster defenses there. The colonies were ramping up their efforts to raise troops. Gradually, the population advantage of the British colonies began making a difference.[23]

In the meantime, the violence on the frontier continued. On April 18, 1758, six Shawnee and four French soldiers captured twelve-year-old Mary Jemison a few miles west of where the town of Gettysburg, Pennsylvania, would be founded a few years later. The rest of her family was killed, and she was taken to Upstate New York and adopted into a Seneca family. She married and remained with the Seneca, receiving the name Deh-he-wa-nis. She had the opportunity to return but chose to live her life with the Seneca, dying in 1833 at the age of ninety-one. She is one example of a captive who chose to remain with their new Native family.

From 1755 to 1758, warfare raged on the frontier from Pennsylvania through Virginia and into the Carolinas, New York and New England. The French had reached the limits of their influence and power by 1758. Both sides had been too weak to strike a decisive blow and knock out the other— yet that was about to change.

Sites to Explore

Ashby's Fort Museum
227 Dans Run Road | Fort Ashby, WV 26719
www.fortashby.org | GPS: 39 30.311, -78 45.923

This fort was built in 1755 to protect area settlers, and there was an engagement there the next year. Today, a reconstructed fort and museum occupy the site.

Fort Augusta and Hunter House
1150 North Front Street | Sunbury, PA 17801-1126
570-286-4083
www.northumberlandcountyhistoricalsociety.org/area-history/fort-augusta-hunter-house
GPS: 40 86.5367, -76 79.5077

This unique museum features a model of the fort in its front yard. The fort is gone, but the well is marked.

One of the most unique historic sites is the model of Fort Augusta at the site of the fort in Sunbury, Pennsylvania. A museum stands just behind the scale model. *Author's collection.*

FORT CHISWELL MONUMENT
GPS: 36 94.8408, -80 93.432

Built in 1758, this fort was defending Virginia's frontier. This was the site where wagon driver Daniel Morgan was punished with 500 lashes. He always claimed that the British miscounted, only dealing 499.

The foundations of the fort and its surrounding buildings were completely covered during the construction of Interstate 77 in the 1970s. A pyramid-shaped monument of sandstone stands about two hundred yards west-northwest of the fort's original location, next to the old chicken house.

The monument is located on East Lee Highway, next to the southbound ramp of Interstate 77 onto Interstate 81. There are no facilities at the site.

FORT FREDERICK STATE PARK
11100 FORT FREDERICK ROAD | BIG POOL, MD 21711
301-842-2155
GPS: 39 36.767, -78 0.409

This site interprets the defense of Maryland's colonial frontier. The fort is a rare example of stone construction from the colonial period, and the site holds many living history events.

Fort Frederick was a massive stone fort built in the classic design with four bastions on the Maryland frontier. The Civilian Conservation Corps rebuilt the fort in the 1930s, and today, it is a state park with a museum. *New York Public Library.*

FORT HALIFAX PARK
570 NORTH RIVER ROAD | HALIFAX, PA 17032
WWW.FORTHALIFAXPARK.ORG
GPS: 40 28.934, -76 55.879

Built in 1756 by Colonel William Chapman, this fort overlooked the Susquehanna River and was one in a line of posts that defended the frontier. A historic marker stands along Route 147, and a park with historic markers preserves the site. There are no facilities at the site.

FORT HUNTER MANSION AND PARK
5300 NORTH FRONT STREET | HARRISBURG, PA 17110
717-599-5751 | WWW.FORTHUNTER.ORG
GPS: 40 20.516, -76 54.585

Built in 1755 along the Susquehanna River to protect the frontier, this fort is long gone. And in the 1800s, a mansion was built on the site. Today, there is a riverfront park with historic markers about the history here.

FORT McCORD SITE
GPS: 39 59.094, -77 46.41

This was the site of a frontier fort raided by Natives on April 1, 1756. Twenty-seven settlers were killed or captured in the raid. A monument marks the spot. The marker is located on Rumler Road, 0.1 miles south of Fort McCord Road. There are no facilities at the site.

McCord's Fort near Chambersburg was one of the settlements attacked during the numerous raids on the frontier. *Author's collection.*

Fort Phillip Davis Site
Welsh Run, PA 17326
GPS: 39 45.571, -77 51.757

The southernmost fort in Pennsylvania, this fortified home was built by Phillip Davis to shelter his and nearby families. Natives raided nearby homes and burned the local church. Today, a historic marker stands off Bain Road near its intersection with Royer Road. There are no facilities at the site.

Fort Shirley Site
U.S. 522, North of Town | Shirleysburg, PA 17260
GPS: 40 18.074, -77 52.449

Built in 1756, Fort Shirley was the jumping-off point for Armstrong's raid on Kittanning. It was also the scene of several Native conferences. Today, a marker notes the site. There are no facilities at the site.

Fort Waddell Site
Route 30 | St. Thomas, PA 17252
GPS: 39 54.671, -77 49.244

This fort was built in 1754 to protect settlers in the region near the Great Cove. A historic marker notes the site. Thomas Waddell fortified his home and offered shelter to his neighbors. It was one of the main private forts in the area. There are no facilities at the site.

George Washington Office Museum
32 West Cork and Braddock Streets | Winchester, VA 22601
540-662-4412
GPS: 39 10.949, -78 10.062

This small building served as Washington's headquarters during the frustrating years he tried to defend Virginia's vulnerable frontier.

HARRIS AMBUSH SITE
SOUTH OLD TRAIL
SELINSGROVE, PA 17870
GPS: 40 48.807, -76 51.256

A party led by John Harris rode north from the Paxton area to investigate in the aftermath of the Penn's Creek raid on October 25, 1755. Near the mouth of the creek, about thirty Natives ambushed them. A monument notes the site. There are no facilities at the site.

INGLES FARM
9 WILDERNESS ROAD | RADFORD, VA 24141
540-267-3153 | WWW.RADFORDVA.GOV/501/INGLES-FARM
GPS: 37 10.3723, -80 58.6270

Sitting on the property of William and Mary Ingles is a replica cabin. Visitation is possible by appointment only.

KITTANNING MARKERS
KITTANNING, PA
GPS: 40 48.813, -79 31.276

This Delaware village on the flat land along the Allegheny River was a launching point for many raids and was targeted by Pennsylvania troops in 1756. Two markers are located at the intersection of Market Street (U.S. 422) and Water Street in Riverfront Park. There are no facilities at the site.

The large village of Kittanning spread out along the flat land along the east side of the Allegheny River. The Pennsylvania troops approached from the right, attacking with total surprise. *Author's collection.*

LETCHWORTH STATE PARK/MARY JEMISON'S GRAVE
1 LETCHWORTH STATE PARK | CASTILE, NY 14427
WWW.PARKS.NY.GOV/PARKS/79/DETAILS/ASPX
GPS: 42 57.0148, -78 5.1170

Mary Jemison's grave was moved to this site when the reservation land where she rested was sold. The grave is marked with a large monument and statue.

MARY INGLES DRAPER MONUMENT
WEST VIEW CEMETERY
1500 FIFTH STREET | RADFORD, VA 24141
GPS: 37 12.1005, -80 58.5806

Standing about a mile and a half from the Ingles farm, this 1909 monument honors Mary using stones from the original cabin. There are no facilities at the site.

MARY INGLES DRAPER STATUE
601 UNRUH DRIVE | RADFORD VA 24141
GPS: 37 7.976, -80 34.868

A statue of Mary Ingles Draper stands in Mary Ingles Draper Cultural Heritage Park in Radford.

MARY JEMISON STATUE
ST. IGNATIUS LOYOLA CHURCH
1095 CHURCH ROAD | ORRTANA, PA 17353
WWW.STIGNATIUSOFLOYOLA.ORG
GPS: 39 55.028, -77 23.723

Shawnee kidnapped the Jemison family near this site, and a statue in front of this church honors Mary Jemison.

Not far from Gettysburg stands this monument dedicated to Mary Jemison, who was taken captive in a 1758 raid. *Author's collection.*

Penn's Creek Massacre Site
GPS: 40 54.329, -77 1.656

A historic marker stands at the site of the Leroy farm in rural Union County, where Natives stuck on October 16, 1755. The event became infamous and remains vivid in local lore from this period. This marker is located at the intersection of Ridge Road (3016) and Dice Road on Ridge Road, south of the town of Mifflinburg. There are no facilities at the site.

Steel's Fort Site
Mercersburg, PA 17236
GPS: 39 48.246, -77 52.195

Reverend John Steel was a Presbyterian minister who built a stockade fort around his church. Refuges found shelter here after the 1755 Great Cove raid. A monument near the church's cemetery marks the site. The marker is located at the intersection of PA 16 and Findley Road. There are no facilities at the site.

Mary Draper Ingles Trail
WWW.MARYDRAPERINGLESTRAIL.COM

This website includes information about historic sites related to Mary and her capture and the war in this area.

FORBES

The slow advance of the new road and the cause of it touched me to the quick.
—*General John Forbes*

By 1758, despite French military success in the Ohio Country and elsewhere, New France's economy could not sustain a protracted war, and trade supplies dwindled. The effects on their Native allies were profound. Dependent on the French for hunting and military supplies, as well as diplomatic gifts, the Natives keenly felt the lack of goods. At the Forks, French troops expanded Fort Duquesne to the east in 1758, constructing a long palisade that enclosed several buildings on the landward side. Crops and livestock were located farther out, beyond the new enclosure.

While fighting against the French, Pennsylvania and Virginia were waging their own war over their unresolved boundary and the western lands they hoped to control. The rivalry nearly undercut the British effort to capture the Forks and remained unresolved until the Revolution twenty years later.

In March 1758, General John Forbes assumed command of the next effort to capture Fort Duquesne, the source of raids on the frontier and the goal of colonial forces since 1754. Forbes relied heavily on his second-in-command, Swiss-born Colonel Henry Bouquet. Forbes had a great deal of administrative work to do but was also suffering from cancer and dysentery. Based in Philadelphia, Forbes could follow the already-cut Braddock Road over the mountains or march directly west across Pennsylvania.[1]

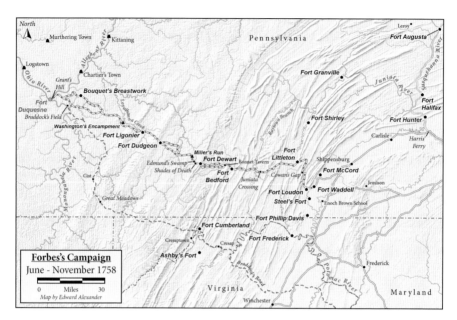

General John Forbes marched his army west, building forts as he went. Approaching Fort Duquesne, they took the upper fork of the road. *Edward Alexander.*

Washington and Virginia officers advocated strongly for the Virginia route, the old Braddock Road. It was already built and was wide enough for wagons and artillery. Washington was also familiar with the area's terrain and its landmarks. More importantly, looking ahead to the postwar years, Washington felt Virginia would benefit from postwar trade and settlement if the Braddock Road was used. If Forbes built a new road west from Pennsylvania, that colony stood to gain.[2]

Washington pushed the limits of propriety when writing to Bouquet in July:

> *I am convinced that a road, to be compared with General Braddock's, or, indeed that will be fit for transportation even by pack-horses, cannot be made....I have been uniformly told that, if you expect a tolerable road by Raystown you will be disappointed for no movement can be made that way without destroying our horses.*[3]

To a friend he privately wrote, "If Colonel Bouquet succeeds in this point with the General all is lost! All is lost by Heavens! Our enterprise ruined." Unfortunately, the letter reached General Forbes, irritating him greatly.[4]

Forbes kept his options open, stating that he was not going to let politics guide his choice; instead, he would use military necessity. The general had Washington's force at Fort Cumberland open the old Braddock Road at the same time that Bouquet's forces were moving west from Fort Loudon, Pennsylvania. It kept the French guessing about the real threat, and it kept an alternate option open if the new route west should prove impractical. Forbes stated, "If what I say is true and those two roads are compared, I don't see that I am to Hesitate one moment which to take unless I take a party likewise which I hope never to do in Army matters." By late July, the matter was settled; the route directly west had its challenges, but it was the more practical route.[5]

Another possible motive, not mentioned by Forbes but certainly on the mind of anyone studying the problem, was that taking Braddock's Road meant the troops would have to pass through the site of Braddock's defeat. It was well known that scores of the slain lay unburied on the battlefield. Passing the site would have been demoralizing to the army.

That summer the army gathered in Carlisle, eventually reaching six thousand in number. The force included men from two regular regiments: the Sixtieth Regiment, known as the Royal Americans, and the Seventy-Seventh, or Montgomery's Highlanders. There were also regiments from Pennsylvania, the Lower Counties (modern-day Delaware, still part of Pennsylvania at the time), Maryland, Virginia and North Carolina. In addition, a contingent of Catawba and Cherokee from the south joined the expedition. Serving with the Pennsylvania troops was Lieutenant Colonel Hugh Mercer. George Washington commanded the First Virginia Regiment, and William Byrd III commanded the Second. It formed the largest concentration of people in the Mid-Atlantic after New York and Philadelphia.[6]

June found General Forbes in Philadelphia, dealing with the monumental challenges of securing supplies and the administrative issues with organizing the army. In the meantime, Bouquet had arrived at Carlisle and was organizing things on the front lines, overseeing the building of the road and supplying the army. Two major challenges were finding good horses and foraging to feed them.[7]

Forbes and Bouquet developed a special relationship while working hundreds of miles apart, with Bouquet writing in French and Forbes replying in English. This trust was a key element in the campaign's ultimate success. Forbes increasingly relied on Bouquet as his health worsened, frequently writing in his letters that he was "tyred."[8]

Colonel Henry Bouquet was a Swiss-born officer who served in the British army. His tactics at Bushy Run are still studied for their brilliance. *New York Public Library.*

Thomas Cressap, an Indian agent for Maryland and an Ohio Company investor, assisted in the supply effort. Cresap gathered supplies in the area near his settlement in western Maryland along the Potomac River and coordinated with the garrison at Fort Cumberland.[9]

As Forbes's army advanced west, they built a series of strongpoints along the way. These served as bases of supply and fallback points if needed. Unlike with Braddock, there was not one single advance; instead, several units leapfrogged as they moved closer to the enemy at the Forks.

On June 8, 1758, Bouquet arrived at Fort Loudon and prepared for the next leg of the movement. In the distance, soldiers could see the first of many ridges they had to cross. On June 14, Bouquet held a meeting with the Cherokee and Catawba here. They were impatient with the slow progress of gathering the army for the campaign and reluctantly agreed to join the expedition. In the meantime, the two Virginia regiments had assembled at Winchester, still hoping to march up the old Braddock Road. With them were troops from North Carolina. Colonel Washington wrote on June 14 of a "French Negro" who had escaped Fort Duquesne and been picked up by his troops. Washington hoped that the "shrewd sensible Fellow" would provide good intelligence on the fort.[10]

On June 22, the army's advance reached Juniata Crossing on the Raytown Branch of the Juniata River (about two and a half miles west of modern-day Breezewood, Pennsylvania). Also in June, the two Virginia regiments and the North Carolina troops moved from Winchester to Fort Cumberland and then to Fort Loudon, the route issue having been settled. In early July, Forbes left Philadelphia for Carlisle. The Seventy-Seventh Highlanders and the Pennsylvania troops moved west toward Fort Littleton. The next objective for the advance was Ray's Town, which was named for a Native trader and is now the modern town of Bedford.[11]

In mid-August, Forbes moved from Carlisle to Shippensburg. At times, he felt better, but his illness dragged on and intensified. He wrote of the "most violent and tormenting distemper" and "pains intolerable." He was fortunate to have the efficient Bouquet working on the front lines.

By this point, Bouquet had reached Ray's Town, where the Pennsylvania and Virginia troops began to build Fort Bedford on June 28. Looming west of Fort Bedford were even more imposing mountains. In addition to the logistical challenges of building the road and supplying the army, Bouquet had to deal diplomatically with the troops from various colonies, British regulars and Native allies. He succeeded, writing, "I have established harmony between the different corps." By the last week of August, the Sixtieth, Seventy-Seventh and Pennsylvania, Virginia and North Carolina troops had reached Loyal Hanna (now Ligonier).[12]

While the bulk of the army moved slowly and concentrated first at Fort Loudon—then Fort Bedford—scouts were actively out west, looking for the best route, carefully scanning the mountains ahead and the swamps beyond them. There were several Native paths that offered possible routes.[13]

West of Fort Bedford loomed Allegheny Mountain, perhaps the toughest ascent the army faced. One British officer, while scouting ahead for a good route, noted it was "very Steep and Stony. I very much doubt whether Loaded Wagons can be got up this Mountain." Yet engineers indeed found a route up the mountainside.[14]

On top of the ridge, the Seventy-Seventh Regiment built a small fortification called Fort Dewart, a sixty-foot-square earthen redoubt. It was a protected place for the men to rest after ascending the mountain. Named for Duart Castle in Scotland, it is the only original fortification still on the route, and it is now located in a private community.[15]

To the west of Fort Dewart the troops encountered the Shades Death, a dark, gloomy forest of pines so dense that sunlight could not penetrate it. Virginia officer Adam Stephen called it a "dismal place." Beyond that, the army entered Edmund's Swamp, where they had to build a corduroy road of logs. Further west, in early August, they reached Miller Run near modern-day Center City, just north of Route 30 and the Flight 93 Memorial.[16]

At a location called the Clear Fields, the army built Fort Dudgeon, another small stopping point and a location that had forage for horses. It stood near Kline's Mill north of Jennerstown but was destroyed by strip mining in the 1900s. Farther west at the Stoney Creek encampment, Pennsylvania soldiers built another fortification and bake ovens to provide fresh bread along the march. Today, the site is noted with a historic marker at Kanter in front of North Star School.[17]

Fort Bedford was the next major post constructed west of Fort Loudon. It was the staging area and jump-off point once Forbes committed to the Pennsylvania route. Today, a reconstructed fort and museum occupy the site. *Author's collection.*

By now, Forbes had moved to Fort Loudon, still in great pain and dealing with administrative issues. He reported to Bouquet the good news of the British capture of Fortress Louisbourg in Nova Scotia in late August. On September 3, troops began to build a fort at Loyal Hanna, or Loyalhannon (Algonquian for "middle stream"), called Fort Ligonier and honoring Lord Ligonier of the British army. Overlooking Loyalhanna Creek, the fort was two hundred feet long on each side. Built in the classic design with four bastions, its walls consisted of horizontal logs that were seven feet high, ten feet thick and filled with earth. The fort included storehouses, a cattle pen, a hospital, a blacksmith shop and an underground powder magazine. There were outer defenses and batteries around the main fort for added protection.[18]

At Fort Ligonier, an impatient Major James Grant proposed striking forward to quickly capture Fort Duquesne. Bouquet reluctantly agreed. Forbes arrived at Fort Bedford a week later on September 15. The next day, news arrived of the late-August capture of Fort Frontenac on Lake Ontario, a key French fort (now Kingston, Ontario).[19]

As the leaves began to change that fall, Robert Kirk, a soldier in the Seventy-Seventh Highland Regiment, noted that "the trees and the Indians were of the same color" and that in the woods "at that season they have a full view of you, but you have the least idea of them."[20]

For his expedition, Major Grant took 860 men from the Seventy-Seventh, the Sixtieth, Virginians, Delawareans, Marylanders, Pennsylvanians and the Cherokee. He was to advance to a hill overlooking Fort Duquesne, and if he was not discovered, he was to strike at the Native camps outside the fort and fall back and set an ambush for them. If he was discovered, he was to retreat to Fort Ligonier. They left on September 9.[21]

On September 13, Grant's forces reached a hill less than a mile from the Forks. Undetected so far, at this point, Grant made several mistakes. It was a comedy of errors, as men went forward at night, got lost and returned without making contact with the enemy at the fort. Grant then sent another force forward with dawn coming. Making it to the outskirts of the fort, they set fire to a supply building outside the walls. In the meantime, Grant sent a force back to prepare an ambush and then had his drummers play as daylight broke. The startled French garrison awoke, and along with their Native allies, they streamed out to attack.[22]

Robert Kirk recalled the unfolding disaster. "We began our attack, by posting three companies over against the gates of the Fort with orders to rush in as soon as they heard the main body attempt the walls. That we might the better distinguish our own people every one had a white shirt over his coat."

He notes that when the French and Natives learned of their presence, a group of Natives came up both the Alleghany and Monongahela Rivers, "and thus, when we least expected, attack'd us in the rere, and the whole strength of the garrison in our front. The three companies before mention'd, stood firm a long time, and by their regular platoon firing annoyed the enemy greatly. But by their superiority and repeated attacks, those brave handful was at length broke and obligate to retreat in confusion to the main body." He continued, "It is impossible to describe the confusion and horror which ensued, when all hopes of victory was gone. We were dispersed here and there, for my part I cannot inform the reader, how affairs went with my fellow soldiers, for I was pursued by four Indians, who fired at me several times, and their shot went through my cloaths, one of them, however made sure, and wounded me in the leg."

Grant himself, along with 270 men, was taken prisoner, and the remnants retreated the fifty miles back to Fort Ligonier. Forbes considered it a major setback. In the days afterward, Bouquet and de Ligneris exchanged letters, with Bouquet asking if he could send supplies to help the captured British officers. De Ligneris replied that they had already been sent onto Montreal and assured they would be well cared for.[23]

To follow up on their success, a French and Native raiding party of about 590 struck Fort Ligonier on October 12; 500 men from the garrison of 1,500 came out to repulse them with support from the fort's artillery. Captain Charles Aubry led the French force, who managed to make off with some of the garrison's horses.[24]

Forbes himself arrived at the fort on November 2, still in a litter. Ten days later, an incident occurred that nearly cost Colonel Washington his life. Two groups of British troops fired into each other by mistake, and Washington rode between the lines, knocking up muskets with his sword. Washington wrote that he was in "imminent danger," as he was "between two fires, knocking up with this sword the presented pieces." Washington

This marker on the Allegheny County Courthouse in downtown Pittsburgh notes that the hill was the site of Grant's defeat in September. *Author's collection.*

had come very close to death, as he had at Braddock's defeat, Jumonville Glen, Fort Necessity and the return trip from Fort Le Bouef.[25]

At Fort Duquesne that November, the French lost many of their Native allies. The Great Lakes tribes, the Pays den Haut, departed with the coming of winter and the end of the campaign season. Having defeated Grant, many felt that, as they had done with Braddock's column, the British were finished for the season and would retreat. Supplies were also running low at the fort, and the Natives could not rely on the French for food or gifts.

By mid-November Forbes's entire army of about six thousand troops was assembled at Fort Ligonier. On November 11, Forbes held a council with all of his officers to discuss whether they should push on or end the campaign for the season. Forbes reluctantly resigned himself to end the campaign with coming winter. They had come close, but the final push to capture Fort Duquesne would have to wait until spring. Then—as it so often happens—things changed quickly. The next day, a few French prisoners were taken after they tried to steal the garrison's cattle. Learning of the weak state of Fort Duquesne and the desertion of many Natives, Forbes decided to push ahead.[26]

On November 14, Forbes divided the army into three brigades, under Colonels Bouquet, Montgomery and Washington. The next day,

Reconstructed on the original site, Fort Ligonier sits above Loyalhanna Creek. *Author's collection.*

Washington, with the First Virginia Regiment, North Carolina, Maryland and Lower County (Delaware) troops, moved out. Following was Archibald Montgomery with the Second Virginia. Bouquet followed with the Pennsylvanians and the Sixtieth.[27]

Fort Ligonier was now the army's main supply base and fallback position, a crucial post along the road. It was attacked twice five years later in 1763, during Pontiac's Rebellion. In March 1766, the fort was decommissioned, and by the 1830s, it was entirely gone. The town of Ligonier grew up and was partially built over the fort site.[28]

The site of the fort drew the attention of archaeologists in 1947 and again in the 1960s. Using maps, researchers were able to locate the site of the fort and excavate the foundations of its buildings and fortifications. Archaeologists assembled an amazing collection of artifacts, which has proved invaluable to researchers of the period. Buttons, buckles, leather cartridge boxes, shoes, tools, canteens, saddle parts, utensils, wagon parts, cups, ceramics and more from the site have been of immense value to scholars and reenactors. Fort Ligonier emerged as one of the most important eighteenth-century military archaeological sites. In addition, much was learned of the garrison's diet from the cow, sheep, pig and deer bones found at the site.[29]

Native diplomacy played a crucial role in the Forbes campaign. The key breakthrough came from Easton, Pennsylvania, nearly three hundred miles away from Fort Duquesne. Here, in the town square, a council with representatives from the various Ohio Country tribes met with Governor William Denny, Conrad Weiser and other colonial officials starting on

October 7. Key negotiators on behalf of the Delaware included Kutaikund, Tamaqua, Shingas, Pisquetomen and Teedyscuing.

Pennsylvania agreed to return some lands to the Leni Lenape, respect their hunting grounds in the Ohio Country and not to establish settlements west of the mountains (this was later repeated by the British government in the Proclamation of 1763). Governor William Denny of Pennsylvania also agreed to negotiate directly with the Delaware rather than go through the Six Nations (Iroquois/Haudenosaunee). The Leni Lenape agreed to stop supporting the French. An estimated five hundred Natives attended this council, and the agreement was concluded on October 26, 1758.

Word reached Native diplomat George Croghan that the Natives of the Ohio Country were "very much distressed for Provisions," and "the Indians, to whom large presents cannot be made, as the stores are empty, begin to dislike going out to fight." He worked with other Indian agents to spread the news of the breakthrough treaty.[30]

Moravian missionary Christian Frederick Post was respected by the Delaware, as he had lived with them and spoke their language. He journeyed west with the news of the treaty and extended offers of renewed trade with Pennsylvania. Post met with several key Native leaders in August and September 1758.[31]

Post ventured deeper into the frontier, stopping at Kuskuski at the junction of the Shenago and Mahoning Rivers (modern-day New Castle, Pennsylvania); he even went to the north bank of the Allegheny River across from Fort Duquesne. There, at the seat of French power in the region, he spoke to the Natives about peace with Pennsylvania and the British. Many began to openly shun the French. Incredibly, the French were unable to prevent this emissary from coming to their very doorstep.[32]

The Easton conference was a resounding success for the British, as the Delaware, Shawnee and Mingo agreed to terms of friendship with the English. Colonel Bouquet called it "the blow which has knocked the French on the head."[33]

While the diplomatic maneuvering was underway with the Leni Lenape, Shawnee and Mingo of the region, an influx of Great Lakes tribes arrived at Fort Duquesne. These supporters of the French included the Ottawa, Chippewa, Potawatomie and Wyandot (the Pays den Haut). Many had come from as far as Fort Detroit, and their purpose was to aid the French in stopping Forbes.[34]

The last leg of the advance saw Forbes's unit leapfrog toward Fort Duquesne. On November 15, the advance left Fort Ligonier. Washington's

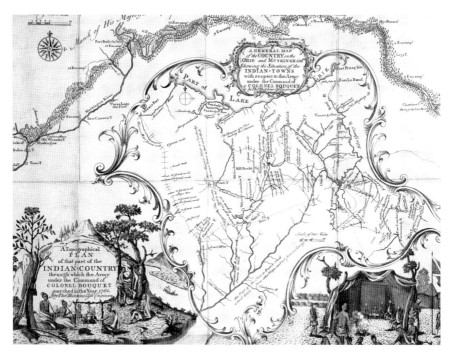

This British army map shows the area crossed by Bouquet in 1764 to subdue the Natives. It also shows other important landmarks, like Braddock's battlefield and various fort sites. *New York Public Library.*

regiment camped near the modern St. Vincent College near Latrobe. On November 22, Colonel Bouquet's troops camped near the future site of Boyce Park in Monroeville. Forbes arrived the next day, made final preparations for the last leg and issued the instructions to beware of an ambush and to always have weapons ready.[35]

Serving as an officer with the Pennsylvania troops, William Trent guided the advance and helped advise the route toward the Forks. Perhaps he was anxious to see the British reclaim what he had held four years earlier.[36]

Small garrisons of around fifty men each were kept at the small redoubts like Fort Dewart, Fort Dudgeon and Stoney Creek to protect supply convoys as they went forward. Work parties were also active between these posts, rebuilding the road, adding bridges and keeping the route in good repair—all things that were not done in the Braddock expedition. Washington issued strict order for his detachment as they neared the French fort, preparing for an ambush and marching with flankers out in front of the main column.[37]

Deserted by the Natives, with an overwhelming force bearing down on them, the French abandoned the symbol of their control of the Ohio Country on November 24. Remaining trade goods were sent to the Natives, and the fort's artillery was loaded onto bateaux and sent west on la Belle Riviere to the Illinois Country. Using the fort's gunpowder supply, they set the post on fire and left. The explosion sounded the end of French dominance at the Point.[38]

With the smoldering ruins of Fort Duquesne behind him, Captain de Ligneris led about three hundred troops north up the Allegheny River to Fort Machault. From there, the troops were dispersed among this fort and Forts Le Boeuf and Presque Isle for the winter. Ligneris fully intended to descend the river in the spring and recapture the Forks. French control of the Forks, having lasted only four years, came to an abrupt end.[39]

Yet other events intervened, namely the English attack on Fort Niagara, a critical link in the long supply line back to Montreal. With the wider war turning against the French, Ligneris abandoned the forts of the Ohio Country between August and September 1759, taking the troops north, back over the portage they had worked so hard to build five years earlier.[40]

On the evening of November 24, at a camp called Bouquet's Breastworks along the Old Frankstown Road in the modern eastern suburbs of Pittsburgh, Allied Native scouts reported to Bouquet that "they had discovered a very thick smoak from the Fort…a few hours after they sent word that the Enemies had abandoned their Fort after having burnt everything." A Pennsylvania officer also noted, "We were informed by one of our Indian scouts, that he had discovered a cloud of smoke above the place, and soon another came in with certain intelligence, that it was burning and abandoned by the enemy." Unknown to both sides, the French were passing up the Allegheny River just a mile north of the British camp.[41]

At daybreak on November 25, the army marched through snow the last twelve miles to the Point. William Trent, George Washington, Henry Bouquet and John Forbes looked out on the ruins of Fort Duquesne. It was both a thrilling and desolate scene; after laboring for months to capture the Point, they had succeeded, yet it was a cold, cheerless day at the Point, with the dark rivers flowing by and the mountains towering on all sides.[42]

The French had left nothing behind, so there were no captured supplies to be had. The British army had no tents or other shelter from the weather, so they camped at the Point as best they could. They also had no fortification in case the enemy struck back, and they were low on supplies. Forbes wrote that they had finally conquered "that nest of Pirates which has so long harboured the murderers and destructors of our poor people." This was perhaps the first reference to pirates in the future city of Pittsburgh, now the name of the city's professional baseball team.

Among those scouring the smoldering ruins were two men who were destined to meet again in twenty years. Colonel Hugh Mercer and Captain John Haslet with the Second Pennsylvania were both Scottish immigrants who were at the Point that day. Both later fought with the Continental army in the Revolution, and they were killed on the same day at the Battle of Princeton during the Revolution in 1777.

Perhaps the first Thanksgiving held in western Pennsylvania can be dated to November 26, 1758, when a British soldier noted that Forbes ordered "a Day of publick Thanksgiving to Almighty God for our Success." Forbes did not have long to relish his hard-fought victory. Returning to Philadelphia after an arduous journey back over the road through the mountains, he died on March 11, 1759, at the age of fifty-one, and he was buried in Christ Church.[43]

Chaplain Thomas Barton of Forbes's army wrote, "I have the Pleasure to write this Letter upon the Spot where *Fort Duquesne* once stood, while the *British* Flag flies over the Debris of its Bastions in Triumph. Blessed be God, the long look'd for Day is arrived, that has now fixed us on the Banks of the Ohio!"[44]

Forbes's army had triumphed, but it was a near-run thing. Forbes himself was gravely ill, and there were intercolonial rivalries, tensions between the British and colonists, uncooperative weather and fear that their Native allies would not remain committed. Despite all this adversity, they had succeeded.

Having seen the Forks of the Ohio River fall back into British hands and with no possibility of advancement in the British military, Washington returned to Mount Vernon, positive that his days as a soldier were behind him. He delved into politics and was elected to Virginia's House of Burgesses. He then married wealthy widow named Martha Dandridge Custis.

There was unfinished business that the British had to attend to at the Forks. The dead from Braddock's defeat, eight miles away, remained unburied after three years. Just three days after taking the Point, on November 28, Forbes sent troops to the battle site.

Accompanying the party was Major Sir Francis Halkett, whose father, Peter (the regimental commander of the Forty-Fourth Regiment), and brother were both killed in the action. A Native who had been in the battle guided the group down the Monongahela River to the site.

Beneath a massive tree that the Native remembered were two skeletons. Recognizing the misshapen teeth of his father, Francis realized he had found the remains of his father, Peter, and his brother James. He buried them both in a grave and laid a highland plaid over it.

The burial party gathered the other remains as best they could, as the bodies had been exposed to the elements for three years and animals had scattered the remains over a wide area. After digging a mass grave and firing a volley in respect, the somber group returned to the Point. Another group went to Grant's Hill to bury the dead that still littered the ground from the September battle. The first actions by British troops at the Point had been the melancholy visits to these sites of prior defeat.[45]

Gradually, a community began to spring up at the Point, and it was called Pittsburgh, after Prime Minister William Pitt, the architect of British victory in the war. Colonel Hugh Mercer stayed behind with two hundred Virginians and Pennsylvanians at the Forks, while the rest of the army departed for the east and went back over the mountain. Bouquet ordered Mercer to build a redoubt that winter. It has been called Mercer's Fort, but it never formally had a name. Located along the Monongahela River, the post included a council house for Native meetings, as well as unburnt logs salvaged from Fort Duquesne. Thus, the British hold on the prize was tenuous and fragile that winter of 1758–59.[46]

Mercer's Fort was quite small, with barracks built into its walls. Mercer had fought with the Scottish rebels at Culloden before moving to Virginia to participate in the Kittanning raid. The troops in the garrison used leftover corn and wheat they salvaged from the fields the French had planted around Fort Duquesne.[47]

General John Stanwix arrived on August 29, 1759, with orders to begin constructing a larger and more permanent post. Work on Fort Pitt began on September 3. Stanwix was sixty-nine years old and arrived after completing a fort in Upstate New York. Finished in 1762, Fort Pitt became a center for Native trade, as Natives brought furs and pelts to exchange for goods brought by traders from the east.[48]

Fort Pitt was the largest British fort in North America, built at a cost of £100,000, or $20.5 million. Its walls were between 188 and 272 feet long, 15 feet tall at the base and 7.5 feet thick at base, tapering to 5 feet thick at the top. The land side was reinforced with brick, while the water sides were covered with sod.

Prime Minister William Pitt implemented new strategies that won the war for Great Britain. Pitt was a champion of rights for Americans, and many towns and counties are named in his honor, the most famous of which is Pittsburgh, Pennsylvania. *Benson Lossing.*

It required sixty-six thousand cubic yards of dirt to be moved. Fort Pitt dwarfed Fort Duquesne, which could have fit within one of the newer fort's bastions (corners). Soldiers were instructed to keep animals from grazing on the sod, which would weaken the walls.[49]

According to the *Pennsylvania Gazette* in March 1760, Fort Pitt mounted eighteen guns and could accommodate one thousand men (though it never would). The paper noted, "It may now be asserted with very great truth, that the British dominion is established on the Ohio." The Natives noted this, too.[50]

Although the Natives of the Ohio Country were glad of the English victory, they insisted that they not stay. They did not want to see permanent English settlement in the area. Like Natives' support of the French the previous four years, their decision to support the British was a largely involuntary choice. One Delaware chief said, "If the English would draw back over the mountain, they would get all the other nations into their interest, but if they staid and settled there, all the nations would be against them."[51]

Following up on their victory, the English occupied the abandoned post of Fort Machault, where they built Fort Venango, and built new forts at the sites of Fort Le Boeuf and Presque Isle. Small garrisons of just a handful of men occupied these scattered posts.[52]

The two British thrusts into the Ohio Country have survived into the twenty-first century as Route 40 (Braddock's Road) and Route 30 (Forbes Road). Route 40 is also known as the National Road, the first federally funded highway, and Route 30 is nicknamed the Lincoln Highway in honor of the sixteenth president. The old roads have been straightened and realigned, but in many places, they follow the original route exactly. In some places, old segments remain, relegated to local traffic.

Downtown Pittsburgh has changed a great deal over time; the shoreline is lower, and several heights, including Grant's Hill, were leveled in the 1910s. When urban renewal transformed downtown Pittsburgh in the 1960s, the new bridges built to carry automobile traffic around the Point were named the Fort Duquesne and Fort Pitt Bridges. Many other landmarks in the city recall these early events. The city streets include Forbes Avenue, Stanwix Street, and others. For over sixty years, the city's major league baseball stadium and home of the Pirates was Forbes Field. The Steelers football team also used this stadium for many years.[53]

Archaeological studies done at the site of Fort Pitt from 1964 to 1965 uncovered one of the fort's bastions (corners). It consisted of a stone foundation with brick in English bond above. This was reconstructed on the landward side. Point State Park was developed at the Point as part of the city's urban renewal project.[54]

The Forks of the Ohio River, which empties into the Gulf of Mexico, is one of the most strategic and picturesque sites in North America. It is the center of the city of Pittsburgh and the scene of much history following the war.

SITES TO EXPLORE

ARMY HERITAGE CENTER
950 SOLDIERS DRIVE | CARLISLE, PA 17013
WWW.ARMYHERITAGE.ORG
GPS: 40 20.6836, -77 16.0459

Forbes's army gathered in Carlisle for its march west, and the United States army has deep roots in Carlisle. The Army Heritage Center includes exhibits, archives and outdoor displays of vehicles, equipment and fortifications from the colonial through modern periods.

COMPASS INN MUSEUM
1386 ROUTE 30 EAST | LAUGHLINTOWN, PA 15655
WWW.COMPASSINN.ORG
GPS: 40 21.1873, -79 19.8937

Located not far from the Forbes Road and housed in an old stagecoach stop, this museum preserves the local history of the Ligonier Valley.

COWAN'S GAP STATE PARK
6235 AUGWHICK ROAD | FORT LOUDON, PA
717-485-3948
WWW.DCNR.STATE.PA.US/STATEPARKS/PARKS/COWANSGAP
GPS: 39 99.8837, -77 92.073

Forbes followed a previously cut road north from Fort Loudon and over Tuscarora Mountain at Cowan's Gap. Today, a state park preserves the terrain encountered by the British. The Tuscarora Trail follows the Forbes route.

This marker in the town square at Easton, Pennsylvania, notes the many historic events that took place here. Among the most important was the conference with the Delaware Natives that brought them to the British side in 1758. *Author's collection.*

Easton Square
GPS: 40 41.466, -75 12.558

This was the location of the signing of several important Native treaties, one of which, in 1758, secured the alliance of the Delaware and ended their attacks on the Pennsylvania frontier. This marker is located on Center Square in Easton, Pennsylvania. There are no facilities at this site.

Forbes Grave
Christ Church
20 North American Street
(On Second Street, above Market Street)
Philadelphia, PA 19106
www.christchurchphila.org
GPS: 39.950689, -75.143637

After returning to Philadelphia, Forbes passed away on March 11, 1759, at the age of fifty-one. There is a marker for him in a chancel in Christ Church, one of the city's most prominent colonial houses of worship, and he rests in the churchyard.

FORT BEDFORD
110 FORT BEDFORD DRIVE | BEDFORD, PA 15522
814-623-8891 | 1-800-259-4284
WWW.FORTBEDFORDMUSEUM.ORG
GPS: 40.019565, -78.503536

A reconstructed fort and museum overlooks the Juniata River in downtown Bedford. This was the jumping-off point for the next move over the mountains and into dangerous territory. The museum highlights the history of the French and Indian War and the Bedford area. Among the important artifacts held here is a rare 1758 British flag.

FORT DEWART
FOLMONT@VERIZON.NET
GPS: 40.036791, -78.763764

Built by Highlanders during Forbes's march, this earthen fort still stands at the crest of Allegheny Mountain, west of Bedford and just north of Route 30. The fort is located on private property, but it is open by appointment as of this writing. Visitors should contact the Folmont Property Owners Association.

FORT LIGONIER
200 SOUTH MARKET STREET | LIGONIER, PA 15658
WWW.FORTLIGONIER.ORG
GPS: 40.240849, -79.237862

Fort Ligonier has been carefully reconstructed, and the museum features artifacts recovered from archaeological digs. Fort Ligonier's artifact collection is world-famous, and the museum covers the entirety of the Seven Years War, from North America to Europe and Asia. In addition, visitors get a good appreciation of the challenges Forbes and Washington

Fort Ligonier was a key point for Forbes's army to gather in the fall of 1758. The fort has been reconstructed on its original site, and the museum displays many artifacts found during archaeological studies. *Author's collection.*

faced while marching over the Allegheny Mountains and maintaining their supply lines. It was here that Forbes made the critical decision to push on to Fort Duquesne in the fall of 1758.

FORT LITTLETON/LYTTLETON
30437 GREAT COVE ROAD | FORT LITTLETON, PA 17223
GPS: 40 3.804, -77 57.667

Established in 1755 by Pennsylvania in response to the Native raids following Braddock's defeat, this small stockade fort was a garrison site during Forbes's march. Today, a historic marker notes the site. There are no facilities at this site.

FORT LOUDON
1720 NORTH BROOKLYN ROAD | FORT LOUDON, PA 17224
WWW.FORTLOUDOUNPA.COM
GPS: 39.896601, -77.886672

This was the first of a string of forts built for the British army. Today, Fort Loudon is reconstructed on the original site. The grounds are open daily, and historic markers tell the story of the events that occurred there. The fort's motto, "Built by Pennsylvanians in 1756, Attacked by Pennsylvanians in 1765," refers to its history of defending the frontier during the war and the growing hostility toward British troops afterward.

Today, at the Fort Loudon historic site, visitors can explore a full-size reconstructed fort. There are several historic monuments and markers on the grounds, and the site hosts special events throughout the year. *Author's collection.*

Fort Pitt

See page 34.

Grant's Hill
Pittsburgh, PA
GPS: 40 26.35, -79 59.805

Grant's Hill in downtown Pittsburgh has been leveled and is now occupied by the Allegheny County Courthouse. A historic marker is on the northwest side of the building at the intersection of Grant Street and Fifth Avenue.

Heinz History Center

See page 99.

Jean Bonnet Tavern
6048 Lincoln Highway | Bedford, PA 15522
WWW.JEANBONNETTAVERN.COM
GPS: 40.042368, -78.560658

This stone building possibly dates to 1762, and Forbes's army passed by the site. Historic markers are located on the grounds. Enjoy a meal and drink in this historic tavern.

Old Bedford Village
220 Sawblade Road | Bedford, PA 15522
WWW.OLDBEDFORDVILLAGE.COM
GPS: 40 4.0566, -78 50.6664

This historic site just north of downtown Bedford showcases historic buildings and features demonstrations of early frontier skills and crafts.

Shawnee State Park
132 State Park Road | Schellsburg, PA 15559-7300
WWW.DCNR.PA.GOV/STATEPARKS/FINDAPARK/SHAWNEESTATEPARK/
PAGES/DEFAULT
GPS: 40 2.622, 78 63.552

Four miles of the original road pass through the state park and can be walked as part of a hiking trail. Washington and his troops passed through here on October 15, 1758.

Somerset Historical Center
10649 Somerset Pike | Somerset, PA 15501
WWW.SOMERSETHISTORICALCENTER.ORG
GPS: 40 7.0387, -79 8.0963

This historic site has a collection of buildings representing the area's early history and preserving its traditional architecture, farming and cooking for a taste of what life was like for early settlers who followed in the path of Forbes's army.

Thomas Crossroads Marker
Intersection of Old Forbes Road and Gravel Hill Road
GPS: 40 14.408, -79 11.894

Here in the modern community of Thomas Crossroads is a stone monument and metal marker for the original road. The site is just east of Ligonier. There are no facilities at this site.

Two lone markers stand in the countryside noting the route of the Forbes Road, just east of Ligonier. *Author's collection.*

Sigal Museum and Northampton County Historical Society
342 Northampton Street | Easton, PA 18042
610-253-1222 | www.sigalmuseum.org
GPS: 40 69.1015, -75 21.0729

This museum explores the history of the region, with exhibits on the important Native treaties negotiated on the nearby square.

8

PONTIAC'S WAR

"They attacked us early, and under Favour of an incessant Fire,
made Several bold Efforts to penetrate our Camp."
—*Colonel Henry Bouquet at Bushy Run*

Fully intending to retake the Forks and reassert their authority in the region, the French collapsed unexpectedly quickly in the Ohio Country. Events elsewhere influenced the war here. In July 1759, the British took Fort Niagara, cutting off the supply link to Canada, and the posts in the Ohio Country withered on the vine.

De Ligneris had assembled hundreds of warriors and intended to move down the Allegheny River from Fort Machault to attack Fort Pitt that spring. Instead, he was diverted to help the Niagara garrison, where De Ligneris was killed and his force routed. The military defeats, along with lack of trade goods, caused more Natives to desert the French, who withdrew from Forts Machault, Le Boeuf and Presque Isle in August 1759. British troops moved north from Fort Pitt to occupy the site of the French forts, building new ones on top of the ruins of the old (and renaming Machault Fort Venango).[1]

In September, a large British army defeated the French at Quebec and subsequently occupied the city. Montreal fell to the British in September the following year. New France had been conquered.[2]

British forces moved farther west, occupying French posts across the vast Great Lakes region. Ottawa leader Pontiac confronted the British when they arrived at Fort Detroit in 1760, demanding to know why they had come to

Montreal was the other large French settlement in Canada after Quebec, and supplies for the Ohio Country came directly from here. *New York Public Library.*

Ottawa territory, already showing the sprit that would animate his leadership in the next round of conflict to come.

Soon, issues of trade and diplomacy darkened the relationship between the British and Americans—and the Natives. With the war over, the British demanded captives be returned, a central part of their diplomacy that clashed with Native understandings of warfare. The Natives insisted, with honesty, that many wanted to stay with their adopted families and said they would not force them to go back to the settlers.[3]

A peace treaty followed in 1763, by which France ceded its North American territory to Britain. Authorities in London and in the American colonies imagined their troubles were behind them. In the Proclamation of 1763, American settlers were forbidden to move west of the Allegheny Mountains, reserving this land for the Natives. British troops withdrew from the region but left small garrisons at the various forts scattered from the Great Lakes to western Pennsylvania.

General Robert Monkton of the British army wrote, "It is time now that the Indians, should live by their Hunting, & not think that they are always to be receiving Presents." His thinking, widespread among British leaders, shows a clear misunderstanding and underestimation of the importance of gifts in diplomacy. General Jeffrey Amherst cut spending, including for trade goods and military supplies for the Natives. He also underestimated the potential Native anger—and power.[4]

The Christian missionary Frederick Post recorded a warning from the Delaware chief Keekyscung, a well-respected and seasoned negotiator:

> *All the nations had jointly agreed to defend their hunting place at Allegheny, and suffer nobody to settle there, and as these Indians are much inclined to the English interest, so he begged us very much to tell the Governor, General, and all other people not to settle there. And if the English would draw back over the mountain, they would get all other nations into their interest, but if they staid and settled there, all the nations would be against them, and he was afraid it would be a great war, and never come to peace again.*[5]

A variety of issues contributed to Native unrest in the Ohio Country. White hunters and settlers returned in violation of the treaties made to tribes and the 1763 proclamation forbidding settlement west of the mountains. The British and colonial governments did not attempt to stop it. The British also did not evacuate their garrisons, many of which were located at the site of old French posts. Cutting off trade also hurt the Natives, who had become dependent on European-made clothing and goods for hunting and completing many daily tasks.[6]

Pennsylvania continued to deal with the Iroquois as rulers of the Delaware and not with the Leni Lenape directly, a source of irritation for the Lenape. There were also lingering tensions from earlier land deals and treaties. Settlers from Pennsylvania and Virginia poured in, seeing the Natives as defeated and the lands as open for settlement.[7]

It was not long before the Natives became disillusioned. Early histories of the event called what happened next "Pontiac's Conspiracy," but the Ottawa leader was just one of many who rallied the Natives to resist the British. Guyasuta was another who was ready to revolt and lead the western Seneca against the intruders.[8]

In April 1761, Pittsburgh was a town of about 160 wooden homes outside the massive fort. The brick fort could hold one thousand troops and was ten times the size of Fort Duquesne. With the French threat gone, the Natives wondered why such a massive fort was built in their territory.[9]

Colonel Bouquet issued a proclamation in October 1761 forbidding settlement west of mountains; it also ordered troops to bring violators to Fort Pitt for trial. They even burned the cabins of settlers who violated the orders. But it was not enough.[10]

A map of significant sites from Pontiac's War in Pennsylvania. *Edward Alexander.*

In the meantime, a religious revival swept through Native villages, which contributed to the unrest. A Lenape prophet in modern Ohio urged a purification, shunning trade with the white settlers and urging a return to traditional ways. Native salvation would be achieved by returning to their roots.[11]

When news arrived of the peace treaty with France. British soldiers and officers noted that the Natives were visibly upset. It was now clear that the French were gone for good, the English were here to stay and the Natives had no European allies.[12]

The new war—an outgrowth of the old war—began in the spring of 1763. Natives surrounded and laid siege to the British troops at Fort Detroit on May 9. Hostile warriors appeared in western Pennsylvania as well. Worried about the small forts to the north at Venango, Le Boeuf and Presque Isle, Captain Simon Ecuyer wrote from Fort Pitt, "I tremble for our posts." The British garrisons at the old French forts were too scattered and too weak to defend themselves.[13]

The Natives next struck on June 2 at the fort at Michillimackinak in modern Michigan. About five hundred Ottawa, Sauck and other Natives gathered around the fort and its garrison of thirty-five soldiers. The Natives held a game of baggataway (similar to lacrosse) outside the fort.

The attack was planned brilliantly. Several Native women stood near the fort's open gates with tomahawks and knives hidden under their blankets. When the game ball landed near the gate, the women handed off the weapons to the players, who, in turn, attacked the unsuspecting soldiers. Quickly, the fort was theirs and the surviving garrison taken prisoner.

Fighting then spread to posts in western Pennsylvania. On June 16, Natives attacked and set fire to Fort Venango, killing its fifteen-man garrison. Two days later, they struck at Fort Le Boeuf. The defenders managed to escape during the night, making their way to Fort Pitt. On June 20, they attacked Fort Presque Isle, firing at it for two days. The garrison of thirty men surrendered and were taken captive.[14]

Fort Pitt's garrison consisted of only 143 men, not nearly enough to man the walls and offer an effective defense. William Trent, who led the early effort to seize the Forks in 1753, commanded the militia inside the fort. Perhaps he had visions of surrendering the Point again. The Natives arrived outside the fort on July 27 and began firing on it day and night. The small garrison did what they could to strengthen the fort, even using beaver traps on the earthen walls.[15]

Ironically, the only time the largest British fort in the continent was ever attacked, it was attacked by Natives who had no artillery. The Natives fired flaming arrows into the fort, and the garrison's women formed a bucket brigade to extinguish the flames. Captain Ecuyer stated defiantly, "I will not abandon this Post. I have Warriors, Provisions, and Ammunition to defend it three Years against all the Indians in the Woods, and we shall not abandon it."[16]

The British learned what the French had experienced about the Forks: annual spring flooding. Water damaged the fort's water-side walls in 1762 and 1763, so Colonel Bouquet ordered five blockhouses be built to strengthen the fort. These freestanding blockhouses were scattered around the interior of the massive brick fort. They were two stories tall and five-sided, twenty-three feet wide and twenty-six feet deep. The

General Jeffrey Amherst seized the French fort at Louisbourg and then was appointed the British commander in North America. He oversaw the capture of Fort Calliron (Ticonderoga), Niagara and Quebec. Despite his success, he underestimated the Native situation after the war. *New York Public Library.*

blockhouses had a stone foundation, with a wood cornice, gun loops and a brick wall above.[17]

Today, only one blockhouse remains, the only part of the massive Fort Pitt to survive aboveground. It is one of the oldest buildings in western Pennsylvania—and certainly the oldest in Pittsburgh. Somehow, it survived the dismantling of the fort and the industrialization of the Point in the nineteenth century, and it was rescued by concerned women of the city in the twentieth century.

William Trent noted in his journal that blankets from the fort's smallpox patients were given to the besieging Natives as gifts during a parley. Trent recorded, "Out of our regard for them, we gave them two Blankets and an Handkerchief out of the Small Pox Hospital. I hope it will have the desired effect." It was an early use of germ warfare.[18]

As news of the violence reached overall British commander General Amherst in New York City, he wrote to Bouquet, "I am persuaded this Alarm will End in Nothing." Ten days later, he wrote again, "I find the Affair of the Indians, appears to be more General than I had Apprehended."[19]

As the siege went on, Fort Pitt was the only post in Western Pennsylvania to hold out (Fort Detroit was the only other not to fall). Natives harassed the garrison but never made a direct assault on the fort's massive brick walls. Then all went quiet on August 1. Learning that a relief force was coming, the Delaware, Shawnee, Mingo and Huron left to attack Bouquet's approaching column.[20]

Learning of the expedition, the Natives were determined to stop it. If they defeated this force, they could force the capture of the holdouts at Forts Detroit and Pitt. Moving east along the old Forbes Road, they prepared to engage, confident that their hit-and-run tactics would succeed as they had against Braddock and Grant.

Colonel Henry Bouquet organized a relief force and began at Carlisle in July. His force, by the last leg of the journey, comprised 390 men from the Forty-Second Highland Regiment, Seventy-Seventh Highland Regiment, Sixtieth Regiment and some Virginia Rangers. They also brought thirty-two wagons with sixty thousand pounds of flour, most of it meant for the beleaguered garrison of Fort Pitt.[21]

Knowing time was of the essence, Bouquet pushed his small column rapidly. They moved out over the old Forbes Road west from Fort Loudon. Some of the troops of the Sixtieth and Seventy-Seventh had been on this route before, having crossed the mountains under Forbes five years earlier. No doubt, they recognized some landmarks and perhaps reflected on that dangerous march. The Seventy-Seventh was particularly understrength, having just returned from the West Indies and attacking Havana. Many of its men were ill from the grueling Caribbean weather. On July 25, the column arrived at Fort Bedford, rested briefly and departed on July 28.[22]

They reached Fort Ligonier on August 2 and departed the next day. To speed up the march, they left their wagons here, loading as much flour as they could onto 340 packhorses. Another thirty or so of the ill Seventy-Seventy Highlanders were left here with the garrison. It was fifty miles to Fort Pitt, and they were entering enemy-controlled territory.[23]

Up to this point, Bouquet had been following Forbes's route. They moved much faster than that advance five years earlier, since the road was already built, but time was ticking for the garrison at Fort Pitt. Moving beyond Fort Ligonier, Bouquet decided to alter his route and take a different path from a location known as the Parting of the Ways. His goal was to reach Bushy Run Station, a supply depot at modern-day Harrison City, rest briefly and continue on to Fort Pitt. Yet just a few miles short of the station, they were ambushed by Natives while ascending a steep hill.[24]

The Fort Pitt Blockhouse, now a museum at the site of Fort Pitt. *Author's collection.*

Bouquet described the combat as it unfolded: "As soon as they were driven from one Post, they appeared on another." The Natives' hit-and-run tactics were maddening for the British. Private Robert Kirk of the Seventy-Seventh Highlanders (who had escaped captivity and rejoined the British) wrote, "We faced about, and having made a kind of breastwork with the flour bags, waited their approach, when they came close up, we gave them our whole fire, and rushed out upon them with fixt bayonets, the Indians are not very well used to this way of fighting, they therefore immediately took to their heels." Yet as soon as they were driven off, they struck again from another sector.[25]

Bouquet had his men fall back to the hill behind them, Edge Hill. Here, they set up a perimeter and spent an uneasy night surrounded by the Natives. The five-foot-long flour sacks were unloaded from the packhorses and built up to form a shelter for the wounded. The three hundred men on the hill waited for dawn. It was a desperate situation, as there was no source of water on the hill and they knew they were surrounded with no help on the way.

Through the night, the Natives yelled and shouted threats at the British on the hilltop, denying them sleep and creating fear. One voice recognized was that of Delaware chief Keekyscung, who shouted insults in English. The Mingo leader Kiasutha was also there. The Seneca Guyasuta is presumed to have been there as well. The English were surrounded, cut off from water, and the Natives were confident they could overrun them in the morning. Perhaps they had visions of another rout on the scale of Braddock's defeat.[26]

Bouquet, crouching down on the hilltop that night with his officers huddled around him, devised a unique plan. Knowing the Natives were ready to close in for the kill, he proposed that some of the troops should fall back from the perimeter in a feigned retreat. When the Natives charged into the gap, those troops who had withdrawn would swing around and strike them in the flank.

It was risky, but Bouquet saw no alternative; they had limited ammunition and no water and could not say on Edge Hill indefinitely. Incredibly, it worked. The next morning, two light infantry companies on the western side of Bouquet's perimeter fell back at the chosen time, and as they fell back, they moved to the south, where they were hidden from view by the terrain. Here, south of modern-day Route 993, they were joined by a grenadier company and another light infantry company. When the Natives charged into the center of the British position, these four companies emerged and fired into the right flank of the Natives. The Natives returned fire but could not withstand the British charge.[27]

The army's flour bags were unloaded, and the wounded placed behind them for protection. Today, replica flour sacks are on the hilltop at Bushy Run Battlefield, along with a monument. *Author's collection.*

Kirk noted, "The Indians thought we were going to break and run away, and being sure of their prey came in upon us in the greatest disorder; but they soon found their mistake, for we met them with our first fire, and made terrible havoc among them with our fixt bayonets and continuing to push them everywhere. They set to their heels and were never after able to rally again."[28]

The British tactic at Bushy Run was one of most successful small unit actions in all American military history. For that reason alone, Busy Run Battlefield is worth a visit. Fifty British troops were killed, and sixty were wounded, a total of one-third of their force. The Native losses are not known, as they did their best to carry off their wounded and dead. Bouquet estimated their losses were about the same. Modern historians speculate they may have lost about twenty, but we will never know. The bloodied column moved the last twenty-five miles to Fort Pitt, arriving on August 10. The Natives had given up the siege and departed.[29]

Bushy Run Battlefield also has an important Civil War connection. During the 125th anniversary celebration of the battle in 1883, the guest of honor was local veteran General Richard Coulter, who commanded the Eleventh Pennsylvania. Coulter and others were instrumental in preserving the battlefield and establishing a park here. It is one of the best-preserved battlefields from the period.

Bouquet wintered at Fort Pitt and organized new troops and reinforcements. He then led an expedition to penetrate deep into Native territory to the west to break their power and end the war. Departing Fort Pitt on October 3, 1764, the massive force of 1,500 included troops from the Forty-Second and Seventy-Seventh Regiments, as well as a large number of Pennsylvania and Virginia soldiers.[30]

They were moving into a territory with no established roads or fortifications, so they proceeded cautiously. The army moved in a precise order, with guards out ahead and to the flanks. Three days after departing, they passed through the ruins of Logstown, which had previously been abandoned.[31]

Unable to procure ammunition and weapons and already weakened from a decade of warfare, most of the Delaware, Shawnee and Seneca of the region were ready to end the fighting. Bouquet insisted on the return of prisoners taken in raids. This was a particularly hard concession, as the Natives traditionally adopted captives into their families to replace those lost in battle.

For example, Robert Kirk, a Highland soldier captured in Grant's defeat in 1758, described being adopted by one Shawnee family. His new brother said "that about four moons before, they were at war with a neighboring nation called Cherokies, and that in an engagement they had, his brother was killed, but that the good Man, i.e., God, had sent me in his place, and that I should have all he had, and his friends should be my friends, and his enemies mine." He also noted, "It is a custom amongst them…when the father, brother, or other relation falls in the war, the next prisoner taken by the son or bother of the deceased, is adopted in his place and they always pay him the regard due to a father or brother. They used me with so much affection, that at first I could not help regarding hem very much."[32]

At the Muskingum River in modern-day Coshocton, Ohio, Bouquet and the Natives met and agreed on terms on October 17. In the meantime, another British column had reached Fort Detroit, breaking the power of the Natives in that region.

At Muskingum, one woman captive who was released was recognized by a Virginia soldier as his wife, who was, with their infant, taken prisoner in a previous raid. Many captives, having spent years with the Natives, were reluctant to leave, as they had adopted the Native customs and language.[33]

On November 18, the army departed to return to Fort Pitt. Waves of new settlers entered the area, and the town grew up outside the fort. In the next few years, the rivalry between Pennsylvania and Virginia heated up over who owned this territory.

Virginia created West Augusta County, and Pennsylvania established Westmoreland County, both in the same region, with rival courthouses twenty-five miles apart (Fort Pitt and Hannahstown, respectively). By this time, tensions were heating up with the mother country, and the colonies were on the way to revolution.

Fort Pitt was decommissioned in 1772, and its British troops withdrew just as the tensions between Pennsylvania and Virginia were heating up—as well as the growing crisis between the colonies and England. The Sugar Act had been passed in 1764, and the Stamp Act was passed the following year, overlapping with Pontiac's War on the frontier. The Boston Massacre had taken place in 1770.[34]

This marker at the forks of the Muskingum River is the only reminder of the important events that took place here in 1764. Colonel Bouquet moved his army here from Fort Pitt, deep into Native territory, and tribal leaders met him here and agreed to end the war and return prisoners. *Author's collection.*

During the Revolution, two Continental army generals, Edward Hand and William Irvine, tried and failed to establish order and navigate the bitter Pennsylvania-Virginia rivalry. Both left the frustrating assignment in under a year. Pennsylvania and Virginia finally settled their boundary dispute, with the former state acquiring the land, but Pennsylvania recognized the land claims of Virginians who had settled in the region.[35]

After the French and Indian War, the town of Pittsburgh grew up around the Point. The old fort was salvaged for materials, but one blockhouse survived amid the changes and was used as a private residence for over one hundred years. The blockhouse stood amid a growing industrial area, with warehouses and railroad tracks running nearby. It also survived the annual floods that inundated the Point, including the 1936 flood that almost entirely covered it. Today, it is the only original part of Fort Pitt remaining, having amazingly survived amid so much change.[36]

The Daughters of the American Revolution preserved the blockhouse in 1892, rescuing it from likely destruction. By the 1940s, the Point had become a congested industrial area in one of the nation's dirtiest and most

One of the most important terms of Bouquet's treaty—and one of the hardest for the Natives to accept—was the return of prisoners. Many refused to go, as they had become attached to their Native families. *New York Public Library.*

polluted cities. Efforts to revitalize the area took shape after World War II and included the creation of Point State Park and the establishment of Fort Pitt Museum.[37]

In July 1803, Meriwether Lewis arrived in Pittsburgh to have a keelboat built for the expedition. The town was a center for boat construction. Lewis hired men to serve on board, and by October, they sailed west down the Ohio River for the start of the expedition near St. Louis.

Pontiac's War reignited the settlers' fear and hatred of Natives—all Natives. A group that called themselves the Paxton Boys murdered a group of peaceful, Christian Conestoga Natives in December 1763 near modern-day Millersville in Lancaster County. The Paxton Boys also attacked Natives held in the Lancaster jail for their protection. The colonial government called for their arrest, and they marched on Philadelphia but were persuaded to not attack the city.[38]

Pontiac himself never ventured into western Pennsylvania, remaining near Fort Detroit to direct the siege there. Unable to force the fort's surrender or capture it, by fall, the Natives withdrew. By then, the Battle of Bushy Run had been fought and Fort Pitt had been relieved.

The rebellion sputtered out, and Pontiac moved west to the Illinois Country, where he intended to rebuild the coalition of tribes against the English and Americans. Unable to do this, he signed a peace treaty with the British at Oswego, New York, in 1766. He lost much of his influence among the tribes, having claimed more authority than he really possessed. Pontiac was assassinated three years later in the Native village of Cahokia (in modern-day Illinois) by a Peoria warrior seeking revenge for Pontiac having killed his uncle.[39]

Like his predecessor General John Forbes, Colonel Henry Bouquet did not live long after his great victories at Bushy Run and Muskigum. Promoted to the rank of general for his actions in the war, he took command of the Southern District, with his headquarters located in Pensacola, Florida, territory the British had won from Spain at the end of the French and Indian War. Soon after arriving, he caught yellow fever and died on September 2, 1765, just two years after his incredible victory at Bushy Run. He was about forty-five years old. He was buried at the fort's burying ground, which has since been washed away by erosion from the Gulf of Mexico. Today, it is impossible to visit the grave of one of the era's most important figures.[40]

SITES TO EXPLORE

BUSHY RUN BATTLEFIELD
BOX 468 | HARRSION CITY, PA 15644
724-527-5584 | WWW.BUSHYRUNBATTLEFIELD.COM
GPS: 40 35.7654, 78 2.6691

This engagement was pivotal in the English defeating the Natives in Pontiac's Rebellion, which flared up after the close of the French and Indian War. A small English force was able to hold off a Native ambush in a small and desperate battle. The park includes a museum and walking trails.

Enoch Brown Memorial Park
Enoch Brown Road | Greencastle, PA 17225
GPS: 39 82.5855, -77 75.299

On July 26, 1764, three Delaware attacked the log schoolhouse that stood on this site. Ten students and their teacher, Enoch Brown, were killed and buried at the site. Today, a monument stands here. There are no facilities at the site.

This marker at Enoch Brown Park in Fulton County commemorates a Native attack on a school here in 1764. *Author's collection.*

Forks of the Muskigum
Ohio Route 83 | Coshocton, OH 43812
GPS: 40 17.429, 81 52.327

This was the farthest point reached by Bouquet's army in 1764, and here, he met with Native leaders who agreed to submit and return their prisoners. A historic marker stands at the entrance to Lake Park Complex north of Coshocton, Ohio. There are no facilities at this site.

Fort Ligonier

See page 136.

Fort Pitt Museum
601 Commonwealth Place | Pittsburgh, PA 15222
412-281-9284
https://www.heinzhistorycenter.org/visit/fort-pitt/
GPS: 40 35.8673, 79 62.777

As one approaches the Fort Pitt Museum, rivers and mountains dominate the surroundings. Although most of the fort lies under modern highways, reconstructed sections and the museum allow visitors to appreciate the scale of the largest English fort in North America. The site also marks the location of Fort Duquesne and is a must-see for any visitor interested in the French and Indian War in western Pennsylvania. The modern city of Pittsburgh surrounds the site, but the strategic Forks of the Ohio River still dominate this historic spot.

Michael Cresap House
19105 Opessa Street Southeast | Oldtown, MD 21555
301-478-5848 | www.michaelcresapmuseum.org
GPS: 39 54.1857, -78 61.1501

Built in 1764 by a local Native trader and explorer Michael Cresap (the son of Thomas Cresap), this sturdy stone house is now a museum. It sits above a crossing of the Potomac River near a Shawnee village site, Opessa's Town. The home is open by appointment only.

The home of Native trader and explorer Michael Cresap in Oldtown, Maryland, along the Potomac River. *Author's collection.*

Native Nations of the Susquehanna Markers
219 South Front Street | Harrisburg, PA 17104
GPS: 40 15.397, 76 52.734

A series of markers talk about the French and Indian War in the region and the attack on the Conestoga Natives by the Paxton Boys. These markers are located on the grounds of the John Harris Mansion. There are no facilities at this site.

Pontiac Marker
329R North Broadway | Saint Louis, MO 63102
GPS: 38 37.465, -90 11.416

After Pontiac was assassinated in Illinois, his body was brought to the French settlement of St. Louis for burial. It's said he was buried at what was then the edge of town, now modern-day downtown St. Louis. There are no facilities at this site.

9

CONCLUSION

As the war drew to a close, fast-paced and overlapping events unfolded in North America. In 1765, Pontiac's War ended, and that same year, Parliament passed the Stamp Act. Colonial Americans were reveling in their victories and pride in the British Empire, but then, they were suddenly dealing with issues none of them saw coming. There followed a decade of discontent and a gradual shift toward resistance to British policies.[1]

Frontier violence continued even after the Natives submitted to Bouquet in 1764. Settlers along the Forbes Road and on the Susquehanna frontier organized to oppose British regulations that they felt were too conciliatory or encouraged Native raids.

On March 6, 1765, two hundred frontiersmen who called themselves the Brave Fellows, their faces painted black and dressed in Native garb, stopped a military packhorse train at Sideling Hill, located between Forts Loudon and Bedford. They wanted to keep the trade goods out of the hands of the Natives. Local settlers also began to harass the British troops garrisoned at Fort Bedford, Loudon and other posts. They even kidnapped a British officer and broke men out of a military jail.[2]

At Fort Loudon in 1765, British troops of the Forty-Second Highland Regiment clashed with the local vigilante Black Boys led by James Smith (from the nearby community of Black's Town, or modern-day Mercersburg). The Black Boys wanted to prevent trade goods, especially weapons and ammunition, from reaching the Natives. By November that year, the British garrison withdrew, one of the first outright acts of defiance toward British authority in the colony.

Pennsylvania had initially enjoyed peaceful Natives relations in the decades of the late seventeenth and early eighteenth centuries. But ironically, the colony experienced some of the most violent warfare by midcentury, and it so thoroughly eradicated its Native population that few remained by the close of the eighteenth century. There are no Native American reservations in Pennsylvania today.

The French and Indian War resulted in French expulsion from North America. No longer would the colonists have an enemy so close, and soon, they would no longer feel the need for British military protection or presence.

The war gave valuable military experience to colonials like George Washington, Daniel Morgan, John Armstrong, Adam Stephens and others. The conflict resulted in the British incurring a massive amount debt, which they transferred to the colonists, feeling it was only right that they should pay for their own defense. The war united the colonies in common cause for the first time. Previously, their rivalries had kept them divided. They also saw weaknesses in the British military. Many, including leaders like Washington,

The site of Little Crossing of the Casselman River in Grantsville, Maryland. Today, a small state park preserves a stone arch bridge that was built for the National Road in 1813. *Author's collection.*

felt betrayed by the Proclamation of 1763, which cut off western land for settlement and speculation.[3]

Washington himself survived several close calls—at least one in each campaign. He experienced a near-miss by a Native and a fall into the icy Allegheny River in 1753; noted the bullets whizzing closely at the Battles of Jumonville Glen and Fort Necessity in 1754; and at Braddock's defeat in 1755, his coat and hat were full of bullet holes. He also rode between the firing lines during a skirmish near Fort Ligonier in 1758.

Other leaders figured prominently later as well. During the Revolution, the Americans tried to court leaders like Seneca Guyasuta, but he supported the British in the conflict. Known to Washington as "The Hunter," he died around 1794, having seen it all: Washington's journey to the French Forts, the defeat of Braddock and the Natives' near-victory at Bushy Run.

Yet the French and Indian War should not be seen just as a precursor to the Revolution, the event that laid the groundwork for that conflict. The war deserves study on its own merit for its fascinating events and the contributions of those who lived through it. At numerous points, events could have gone the other way with far different results.

Reminders of the National Road are scattered along Route 40, which generally follows the path of Braddock's Road. The toll house in Addison, Pennsylvania, is a museum about the road and the lives of the toll collectors. *Author's collection.*

Following this conflict, the area that is now western Pennsylvania experienced more turbulence with the Revolution and then the Whiskey Rebellion. Prosperity came with the opening of the National Road early in the next century.

The region has much more history. The Legion of the United States, a five-thousand-man force organized to deal with the Natives on the frontier, passed through here. General Anthony Wayne, a well-respected veteran of the Revolution, drilled the Legion and led it west, camping for a time at the site of Logstown on the Ohio River in 1792.

Then a few years later, two army officers, Meriwether Lewis and William Clark, organized an expedition to explore the newly purchased Louisiana Territory. Starting in Pittsburgh in 1803, they moved down the Ohio River, also passing the site of Logstown. Today, a historic marker in Pittsburgh notes the site where they launched their boat, and the city is the eastern end of the Lewis and Clark National Historic Trail, which commemorates the expedition.

In the nineteenth century, waves of immigrants built canals and railroads, mined and drilled and built communities. Industrial and transportation history abounds in the region. During the Civil War, Union troops fortified Pittsburgh as well as mountain passes from possible Confederate attack. In 2001, Flight 93 crashed into a field just a few miles from the Forbes Road in Somerset County.

The area abounds in history, and its scenery is unparalleled. Rugged mountains overlook beautiful valleys of hardwoods, streams and waterfalls. Rocky outcroppings emerge from the forest. Powerful rivers wind through the region. Today, visitors can explore all this history and scenery and enjoy great recreational opportunities, like hiking, skiing, fishing, rafting, riding bike trails, camping and more.

Sites to Explore

Bradford House
175 South Main Street | Washington, PA 15301
www.bradfordhouse.org
GPS: 40 16.8183, -80 24.4956

David Bradford was a leader of the Whiskey Rebellion of 1792–94. Visit his house to learn more about him and the rebellion.

CENTURY INN
2175 EAST NATIONAL PIKE
SCENERY HILL, PA 15360
WWW.CENTURYINN.COM
GPS: 40 8.6002, -80 7.0325

Built in 1794, this is the oldest continually operating inn on the National Road. Its guests have included Andrew Jackson, Lafayette, Henry Clay, James K. Polk and Santa Anna. It also displays the only surviving flag that was carried by the rebels during the Whiskey Rebellion.

The Whiskey Rebellion erupted in 1792 over a proposed federal tax on whiskey. The flag used by the whiskey rebels is on display in the Century Inn in Scenery Hill, Pennsylvania. *Author's collection.*

CONOCOCHEAGUE INSTITUTE
12995 BAIN ROAD | MERCERSBURG, PA 17236
717-328-2800 | WWW.CIMLG.ORG
GPS: 39 74.8164, -77 87.2801

Preserving the history of the German, Welsh and English settlers of the frontier, this historic site includes a genealogy library, an exhibit on frontier forts, relocated historic structures and a garden.

GREAT ALLEGHENY PASSAGE TRAIL
WWW.GAPTRAIL.ORG

This rail trail links Cumberland, Maryland, to Pittsburgh, Pennsylvania, where it connects to the Chesapeake Bay and Ohio Canal. The GAP Trail crosses Braddock's Road and passes by numerous historic sites in the area.

HANNA'S TOWN
809 FORBES TRAIL ROAD | GREENSBURG, PA 15601
724-836-1800 | WWW.STAROFTHEWEST.COM
GPS: 40 34.4229, -79 50.7219

Founded in 1773 along the Forbes Road, Hanna's Town was the first county courthouse west of the Allegheny Mountains, and it was attacked during the Revolution. Today, the historic site features a museum and reconstructed buildings.

LAUREL HIGHLANDS TOURISM
WWW.GOLAURELHIGHLANDS.COM

The southwestern counties of Pennsylvania, the heart of the French and Indian War in the region, are known as the Laurel Highlands. Visitor information and trip planning can be found on the region's website.

LEWIS AND CLARK NATIONAL HISTORIC TRAIL
WWW.NPS.GOV/LECL

The Lewis and Clark National Historic Trail is approximately 4,900 miles long, extending from Pittsburgh, Pennsylvania, to the mouth of the Columbia River, near present-day Astoria, Oregon. It follows the historic outbound and inbound routes of the Lewis and Clark Expedition. The trail had a collection of historic sites, markers and places to visit.

LINCOLN HIGHWAY EXPERIENCE
3445 ROUTE 30 EAST | LATROBE, PA 15650
WWW.LHHC.ORG/LINCOLN-HIGHWAY-EXPERIENCE/VISIT
GPS: 40 29.1401, -79 34.1856

This museum highlights Route 30, the Lincoln Highway, which follows much of the route that Forbes and Bouquet used in the 1750s and 1760s.

Modern Route 30 parallels the Forbes Road. It has been nicknamed the Lincoln Highway, and commemorative signs like this recall the road's twentieth-century history. *Author's collection.*

NATIONAL ROAD HERITAGE CORRIDOR
WWW.NATIONALROADPA.ORG

This website has information on the National Road, which follows Nemacolin's Path. This path was used by Washington and Braddock. The website includes information on touring the road and the historic sites along the way.

APPENDIX A

GEORGE WASHINGTON'S EARLY MILITARY EXPERIENCES

I Do not Feel Myself Equal to the Command.[1]
—George Washington

The game," wrote George Washington, is "pretty near up." As he penned these words in mid-December 1776, his army was on the run. With independence less than six months old, the Continental army had just fought and lost four battles in and around New York City. Washington's men were now fleeing across New Jersey for the safety of the Delaware River, having abandoned much of their equipment: tents, clothing, guns and ammunition. Congress had already fled Philadelphia. To make matters worse, at the end of the month, most of the soldiers' enlistments were up.[2]

Washington acted boldly, striking at Trenton and Princeton, boosting morale and probably saving the rebellion then and there. Washington has been credited as one of the America's greatest generals, achieving remarkable success despite long odds. While he is immersed in myth and popular memory, a closer examination reveals that Washington's French and Indian War experiences and, more specifically, the *type* of lessons he learned from them, prepared him to take on other formidable tasks twenty years later.

Throughout the War for Independence, Washington displayed consistent generalship; he developed these capabilities as a young officer fighting on the frontier. During the French and Indian War, Washington was nearly always outnumbered, his forces were nearly always ill-supplied and he had to work with a legislature that was often unsympathetic to the problems he faced. Waging war in the unsettled frontier meant that supply lines, communications and transportation issues were of major concern. Washington came to rely on councils with other officers, and by operating in hostile areas, he became a meticulous planner with an eye for every detail.

In 1753, Governor Robert Dinwiddie sent militia officer Washington to deliver a message requesting the French troops leave the English-claimed Ohio Territory. On the mission, Washington experienced his first taste of diplomacy and wilderness survival.[3]

At the age of twenty-one, Lieutenant Colonel George Washington began to recruit and organize Virginia militia to march to the Ohio Country. From the beginning of his military career, Washington encountered problems and frustration: recruits were slow in materializing, supplies were difficult to procure and the assembly leisurely reacted to these issues. Colonel Joshua Fry was in overall command of the Virginia militia, but with his sudden death, Washington found himself managing Virginia's war effort. The problems were mainly of logistics, moving and supplying men on the frontier. Roads were nonexistent, the closest settlement was Winchester and the high peaks of the Allegheny Mountains presented major obstacles. Marauding Natives threatened Washington's lines of communication, and the countryside could not sustain his forces adequately. The advance became stalled near a makeshift post he named Fort Necessity.[4]

Washington began the shooting war when he attacked and defeated a party of French soldiers nearby. A larger column, however, surrounded his weak troops and forced his surrender at the hastily built Fort Necessity. The Virginians retreated, leaving the Ohio Country firmly in French hands. With his inability to obtain a commission in the British regular army, Washington resigned from the military.[5]

The following year, his interest in the war was aroused again with the arrival of Major General Edward Braddock and two regiments of English regulars. Braddock contacted Washington, asking him to serve as a volunteer aide. On this expedition, Washington again dealt largely with issues related to supply and transportation.[6]

As Braddock's column moved over the Allegheny Mountains and struggled to build a road through the forest, it became apparent they were moving too slowly. Washington offered his advice: send a light column forward to strike at the fort, while the heavy guns, baggage and remaining troops followed at their own pace. The English major general took the colonial Virginian's advice.[7]

Half King's Rock, largely hidden by brush, is a large rock formation. Here, Tanacharison's Natives camped, and he met with Washington. A modern driveway occupies the site at the base of the rock. *Author's collection.*

During much of the march, Washington was incapacitated with illness but joined the advance as they closed in on Fort Duquesne. On July 8, just miles from the fort, the English ran into a French and Native party. In the ensuing battle, the English were routed, as the troops were unable to maneuver or return fire effectively in the thick forest. Braddock was mortally wounded, and Washington escaped with bullet holes in his coat and hat. Upon returning to Virginia, Washington was hailed as a hero, one of the few officers to escape the battle unhurt.[8]

From 1756 to 1757, Washington served as colonel of the Virginia regiment, responsible for defending the colony's western frontier from Native attacks. The assignment was an impossible one, and in many ways, it prepared Washington for the challenges of the future. The young colonel had to defend a frontier of over three hundred miles with less than one thousand men. His militia came and went, their pay was low and supplies were difficult to procure. Letters for help that were sent to the Virginia Assembly in Williamsburg were met with little success. Washington's defense fell apart as parties of French and Native raiders moved between forts and struck settlements.[9]

Refugees fled from the frontier of Pennsylvania and Virginia to the more settled areas of those provinces. Many communities welcomed them, but the sheer volume put a strain on local resources. *National Park Service.*

During June 1757, for example, Virginia instituted a draft, yet its provisions handicapped Washington's ability to meet the enemy threats. His militia could not leave the colony, and the enlistments were short-term. Desertions were rampant, and morale sank. Culpeper County's quota was one hundred men; eighty arrived, but only twenty-five were armed. Twenty men deserted out of a ninety-man detachment from Fredericksburg. At one point, over one hundred out of four hundred men deserted at Winchester, leaving after they were paid and clothed. Washington could barely equip and train his men before either they deserted or their enlistments expired. His regiment became a revolving door.[10]

The years of border defense are probably the most overlooked of Washington's early military career, but they gave the rising officer invaluable experience in dealing with militia, supplying his troops and working with an elected assembly. In his Winchester headquarters, he learned how to manage a war effort, from raising troops to raising money.

By the summer of 1758, English forces were ready to attempt another expedition to take Fort Duquesne. Brigadier General John Forbes prepared to march on the French fort from Pennsylvania with an army of about five thousand men. Forbes began moving west from Carlisle with three brigades, one of which was commanded by Washington. The expedition was delayed by the assembling of troops from various colonies and the lengthy process of securing funds from jealous governments. Washington certainly must have learned a great deal by watching Forbes deal with these colonial assemblies.[11]

During the Forbes campaign, Washington again faced problems concerning logistics, but he was also given the opportunity to independently command a sizable number of troops. As November closed in, the army faced the prospect of being caught in the mountains in winter, isolated from settlements to the east and strung out piecemeal. The enlistments for many troops expired on December 1, and Forbes boldly pushed them with one last drive. Through a series of rapid marches, the brigades advanced and fortified new positions. Washington's brigade marched, cleared a road and erected works as part of the advance. He reported his progress daily to Forbes and was expected to cooperate with the other detachments. Low on supplies and deserted by their Native allies, the French burned Fort Duquesne and retreated to the north. On November 24, Colonel Washington looked out over the Forks of the Ohio River, an objective that had consumed his energies for the past four years. A new fort was raised over the smoking ruins: Fort Pitt.[12]

George's mind soon turned to other concerns. Following the close of the campaign, he resigned to serve as a representative in Virginia's House of Burgesses, and he also married Martha Custis. Disappointed at failing to achieve a royal commission but satisfied with his service, Washington left the military for what he felt was the last time. In the years after the defeat of France, Parliament began to tax the colonies and tighten regulations. By the 1770s, the colonies were on the verge of revolt. When fighting broke out, it began in Massachusetts, where a force of militia assembled to lay siege to Boston.[13]

Throughout the French and Indian War, Washington dealt with massive logistical problems. Moreover, when confronting enemy forces, he was nearly always outnumbered and relied on militia of questionable quality. During the Revolution, Washington was known as a strict disciplinarian. He came to appreciate rigorous training and drill—it was the only way to mold the kind of men he could depend on when facing British regulars. His order of the day for January 1, 1776, stated, "His Excellency hopes that the Importance of the great Cause we are engaged in, will be deeply impressed upon every Man's mind, and wishes it to be considered, that an Army without Order, Regulation, and Discipline, is no better than a Comision'd Mob."[14]

As he learned during the campaigns led by Braddock and Forbes, councils of war allow a commander to gain the advice of his officers and learn new options. Before every major engagement he launched during the Revolution, General Washington called a meeting of his subordinates to garner their thoughts. While critics denounced this as indecisiveness, Washington felt he could make more informed decisions by consulting his generals.

As a strategic planner, Washington occupied himself with details. Moving men and supplies in hostile territory taught him to plan carefully; no detail

Fort Loudon in Winchester was one of the forts defending the Virginia frontier. Today, the site is identified by historic markers. *Author's collection.*

could escape his attention, as it might prove fatal. Nor was Washington the type of general to direct from the rear. Small unit clashes on the frontier taught him the value of personal leadership and gave him an appreciation for analyzing situations personally. Throughout the Revolution, he was near the front, often in the thick of heavy fighting. He personally reconnoitered the ground at Brandywine, entered the fray to place units at Monmouth and supervised the digging of trenches at Yorktown.

Not only did George have to deal with transporting men, vehicles and supplies in his area of operation, but he also had to work with the Virginia government, which could not appreciate the problems he faced on the frontier. Throughout the Revolution, Washington wrote incessantly to the Continental Congress—he needed supplies, wagons and longer enlistments for his men. One letter stated, "I am persuaded, as I am of any fact that has happened, that our Liberties must of necessity be greatly hazarded, If not entirely lost, If their defense is left to any but a permanent standing Army." Washington had the patience to work with this body, and he also understood that while fighting a war, they were also forging a democracy—and military power must be subordinate to civil authority.[15]

When Congress was faced with the decision to appoint a military commander, there were many to choose from: militia officers, veterans of the French and Indian War and former British generals. Perhaps none were more qualified than Washington, largely because of the types of challenges he faced twenty years earlier. When he encountered massive enlistment, supply and organizational problems, he got right down to business and dealt with them. He knew what to do because he had done this before.

Washington's chief weakness was his inexperience in commanding large bodies of men, and he did make tactical mistakes during the war. His personal determination, combined with an offensive-defensive strategy that sought to fight only on favorable terms, helped compensate for this flaw. Washington's strong character also manifested itself in his effort to instill dignity, honor and professionalism in the Continental army.

YOHOGANIA COUNTY, VIRGINIA: THE BOUNDARY DISPUTE BETWEEN VIRGINIA AND PENNSYLVANIA IN THE OHIO COUNTRY

BY ROB ORRISON

The Forks of the Ohio River and their connection with the Mississippi River drew immediate interest from colonial leaders of Virginia, Pennsylvania and Maryland (not to mention the French). Control of the Forks would mean an economic windfall to the colony that controlled them, as well as the rivers that led west to the Mississippi River and ultimately into the Gulf of Mexico.

The first European settlers along the eastern seaboard of North America sought a waterway to the west and a connection to the Pacific Ocean. Though no such waterway existed, the importance of the major west-to-east rivers were important to the settling of the interior and economic trading with Natives and, later, the other European-based settlements in the west. Rivers such as the Hudson, Susquehanna, Delaware, Potomac, James and others played major roles in connecting the interior of the continent to the Atlantic trade.

As settlement moved westward, finding a trade route via water to the Mississippi River became important. This opened not just trade routes but also land that could be sold or patented for new settlements. The governors of Pennsylvania and Virginia laid their eyes on the important "Forks of the Ohio," where the Allegheny and Monongahela Rivers met to form the Ohio River. The Ohio River, flowing westward, connected to the Mississippi River and south to the Gulf of Mexico.

The colonial governors' pursuits to settle the Forks was also promoted by British leaders, as France was moving south from Canada to settle the area west of the Appalachian Mountains. This could block British expansion westward and threaten the British colonies along the Atlantic seaboard. Many saw the Forks as the key to the west, and both Pennsylvania and Virginia laid claim to this territory.

Virginia's claim to the area (modern-day Pittsburgh) was laid in its royal charter. This claim extended Virginia's boundaries in a continuous line to the Pacific Ocean (including a majority of the modern-day United States). Pennsylvania's claim was based on a line that was five degrees longitude westward from the Delaware River. Both colonies claimed the entire southwestern corner of modern-day Pennsylvania, including Laurel Ridge and, to the south of the Kiskiminetas River, the Allegheny and Ohio Rivers.

In 1748, Virginia's aristocracy took the lead in claiming the Forks of the Ohio River by forming the Ohio Company of Virginia. Leaders in this new land speculation company included a who's who of the Virginia planter elite. Thomas Lee and his brothers Augustine and Lawrence Washington were its founders. Its investors included George Mason, George Washington, Robert Carter III, John Tayloe II and many others. Most importantly, Lieutenant Governor Robert Dinwiddie was also involved as an investor and supporter of the effort. This gave the company the political clout it needed. In 1749, the king granted the new company nearly five hundred thousand acres between the Kanawha and Monongahela Rivers. The company agreed to settle one hundred families in the Ohio Valley within seven years.

The Crown also required the Virginians to establish a fort in the region and provide protection for the settlers. British authorities—like the Virginia colonists—saw this as a good way to curb or stop French expansion southward and eastward from Canada and push the Native tribes farther west, opening up the area and its vast natural resources to the British.

The Ohio Company, working with trappers and explorers such as Thomas Cresap and Christopher Gist to survey the new land, also established trading posts along Native hunting paths. These paths would eventually be turned into roads for future settlers to use. Even with the Virginians quickly making inroads in the Ohio Valley, Pennsylvania officials still claimed that the Forks of the Ohio River were in their colony. Like in Virginia, the western boundary of Pennsylvania was not an established line. This hindered settlement in the area near the Point, as settlers were worried that their land claims might not be recognized if Pennsylvania ended up with legal authority of the area. The Virginia Company was able to establish small posts at Wills and Redstone

Creeks, but the goal of taking firm control of the Forks was still at hand. Within this void, the French moved quickly.

It was no secret to Lieutenant Governor Dinwiddie that the French were moving quickly southward to the Forks. He had received word that the French were establishing a series of forts in the fall of 1753. In response, Dinwiddie sent a young George Washington north to communicate with the French and warn them to stay out of the Ohio Country. Washington reaffirmed Dinwiddie's interest in the area around the Point in a letter written on November 22, 1753: "I spent some time in viewing the rivers, and the land in the Fork, which I think extremely well situated for a fort, as it has the absolute command of both rivers." Washington was quickly rebuffed in his meeting with the French, and upon his return, Dinwiddie knew it was a race to establish a settlement at the Forks.

By February 1754, the Virginians started building a fort they named Fort Prince George at the Forks, but soon, a larger French force arrived and forced the Virginians to leave. They then began the construction of a much larger fort they called Fort Duquesne. As this was happening, Dinwiddie dispatched Washington and a small force to reinforce Fort Prince George. Tragedy struck in May, when Washington attacked a French force at Jumonville Glen, which was quickly followed by a French and Native victory over Washington at Fort Necessity in July. The French and Indian (or Seven Years) War had begun.

The role the Virginians played in the beginning of the French and Indian War cannot be overstated. Virginians lobbied to create a new land grant, created a company dedicated to settling that land grant and now sent military forces to secure the area. Their initiative in the area was beginning to make a difference in the debate over jurisdiction. When a new British expeditionary force was sent to America under General Edward Braddock, it was determined that Virginia would host it. The route Braddock took was much influenced by the work of the Ohio Company. Moving by the same route Washington and others had established, the Ohio Company was hoping to use the road Braddock's men were building as their link to the Forks. This would aid immensely in the settlement of the region. Unfortunately, Braddock's march met a disastrous end on July 9, 1755, in a bloody repulse. Unfortunately for the Virginians, the next British force to make an expedition to the Point under General John Forbes chose a very different route. This route, now known as Forbes Road, was a direct route through south-central Pennsylvania from Carlisle to the Forks. Learning from the mistakes of Braddock, the Forbes expedition was well-planned and expertly executed. In November 1758, the British recaptured the forks for the Ohio Company and once and for all pushed the French out of the Ohio Valley.

Although the expedition cleared the way for active settlement to resume, it was slowed by the Proclamation of 1763. The proclamation limited westward expansion across the Appalachian Mountains, but this proved to be only a temporary delay in the inevitable border expansion. In 1767, another colonial boundary was settled between Maryland and Pennsylvania in the creation of the Mason-Dixon line, but this line did not apply to Virginia's claim north of Maryland in the Ohio Valley, so the dispute continued.

As more settlements were established, both colonies established county governments in the region, many overlapping one another. By 1774, as the American Revolution was in its infancy, armed conflict erupted between the leaders of the Virginia and Pennsylvania settlements. Virginia militia attacked Hannastown, the county seat of Westmoreland County, Pennsylvania, east of the Forks. The militiamen arrested several justices who refused to acknowledge Virginia's claim to the region.

Later in 1774, Virginia lieutenant governor Dunmore conducted a campaign against the Shawnee and Mingo nations. Dunmore wanted to end their attacks on Virginia settlements, and he also wanted to use the occasion to settle once and for all which colony controlled the Forks of the Ohio River. By 1774, the British-built Fort Pitt was abandoned and in ruins. Dunmore ordered a new fort built by the Virginians to be called Fort Dunmore. Pennsylvania quickly rebuked Dunmore's claim to the Forks. Dunmore claimed that since Virginia had built the first fort at the Point and the British fort that replaced it was the Crown's property—and Virginia was a "Crown Colony" (Pennsylvania was a provincial colony)—the property should revert to Virginia.

Before Governor Dunmore and Governor John Penn of Pennsylvania could settle the dispute, more pressing matters forced the issue to be dropped. In 1775, Revolutionary events in Massachusetts reached a fevered pitch, and soon, all the American colonies were united against Great Britain. Governor Dunmore was forced to leave Virginia, and Penn was forced into exile in New Jersey—although he tried to stay neutral after his removal from office. Fort Dunmore was renamed Fort Pitt by the Americans and saw continued use throughout the American Revolution.

In 1776, the Virginia General Assembly created three new counties near the Forks: Monongalia, Ohio and Yohogania Counties, respectively. The war, however, delayed much of the formal development of these county

The reconstructed walls of Fort Pitt show the scale of this massive fort. Inside is the Fort Pitt Museum. *Author's collection.*

governments. In 1779, Congress passed a resolution calling on Virginia and Pennsylvania to resolve their boundary dispute, and in 1780, an agreement was reached, extending the Mason-Dixon line five degrees of longitude, "from the western termination thereof to run and mark a meridian line to the Ohio River." This would define Virginia's northern boundary and Pennsylvania's western boundary.

Both states appointed surveyors, who worked together to set the agreed-upon boundaries. Beginning in 1782 and finalized in 1785, the formal boundary between Virginia and Pennsylvania was established. Soon, counties in the region were reformed and reorganized by both states. Considering the long-standing dispute, the final determination of the boundaries was peaceful.

Virginia's hold on the area around the Forks of the Ohio River was tenuous at best. Two critical things that influenced the colony's difficulty in its control were geography and cultural identity. The remoteness of the area in relationship to Virginia's political influence and economic center in Williamsburg meant the Forks region was largely isolated from two of the

Hanna's Town was the first county seat established by the State of Pennsylvania west of the Allegheny Mountains. The rival courthouse of Virginia in Pittsburgh was just twenty-five miles away. Hanna's Town was astride the Forbes Road. *Author's collection.*

most important foundations that drove prosperity in the colony. Additionally, the geography of the mountains naturally dictated settlement patterns and access to the Ohio Valley. Most Virginians found themselves in the lower Ohio Valley, while Pennsylvanians settled in the upper Ohio Valley. Because of these natural settlement patterns, social and cultural ties in the region of the Forks were more closely tied to Pennsylvania than Virginia. Settlers in the area traced their cultural norms and religious ties to the German and Dutch cultures established in Pennsylvania. The people in the region also had little interest in or support for slavery. It would take one hundred years for the Forks of the Ohio River to fulfill the economic promise the Virginians of the Ohio Company dreamed of—not in the fur trade or with mineral resources but with the power of Pittsburgh steel.

THE WHISKEY REBELLION

One of the most infamous events that occurred in the region was the Whiskey Rebellion. The Constitution was only five years old when the violence broke out in 1792. The region had also only recently been awarded to Pennsylvania following a land dispute with Virginia, and there was still a great deal of lawlessness.

The largest town in the area, Pittsburgh, had fewer than 1,000 residents. Washington County, the epicenter of the revolt, had 272 registered distillers (equal to 1 in every 20 families). Whiskey was everywhere on the frontier; it was used for medicine, traded as a commodity and was a means of payment among the laborers and farmers of the area.

Grain harvested and shipped to markets in the east produced four bushels, but distilled into whiskey, it produced fourteen. The liquid was much more economical to transport to eastern markets for the small family farmers of the region. Whiskey distilled in the region was known as Monongahela rye, as it used rye rather than corn and sweet rather than sour mash. It was unique to this region and became part of the local culture.

The young, cash-strapped federal government needed to raise revenue, and one potential source was a tax on whiskey. Yet the tax hit the small farmers of western Pennsylvania especially hard, as it was 25 percent of the value and had to be paid up front before the product was shipped to market. The new law also required a great deal of record keeping and documentation, a burden to families who distilled small batches on the side as part of their farming. Furthermore, those accused of evading the tax would be tried in Philadelphia, three hundred miles away.

Rumors of the new tax circulated in the area in 1791 and brought protests that summer in towns like Brownsville and Washington, Pennsylvania. In September, a tax collector was attacked, tarred and feathered, and others were robbed, beaten or intimidated by mobs. Opponents of the tax organized and encouraged their fellow distillers not to pay the tax.

The law was passed in May 1792 and was followed by a warning from President George Washington to "desist from unlawful proceedings." Violence continued against tax collectors and government officials, with one collector's home broken into and his records stolen.

Protests mirrored those forms used before the Revolution: liberty poles, public meetings, tarring and feathering, violence and intimidation. In 1793, rebels broke into the home Fayette County tax collector Benjamin Wells twice, both times taking documents and records. Mingo Presbyterian Church in Washington County was a meeting place for many rebels, and here, they plotted their next moves.

In 1794, whiskey rebels continued to use threats to intimidate tax collectors and shot up the stills of those who cooperated with the government. They also robbed the mail headed for Philadelphia to see who was secretly supporting the government.

The only battle of the rebellion took place on July 16, when about five hundred rebels surrounded the home of Allegheny County tax collector John Neville, Bower Hill. Neville and a small force of army soldiers and enslaved people defended the home and were forced to surrender. Bower Hill was then burned by the rebels.

Dissatisfaction had spread to western Virginia (modern-day Morgantown, West Virginia) and western Maryland (around Hagerstown) as well. Yet the rebellion there lacked a strong single leader and instead comprised a loose coalition at the local level.

In July 1794, about seven thousand rebels organized to march on Pittsburgh, which they felt was supporting the government. The rebels met at Braddock's Field (the site of the 1755 battle and a local landmark) to march into the town. Pittsburgh residents sent food and drink to placate the rebels, and the town's community leaders assured the rebel leaders that the town was not a threat to them. The rebel army proceeded into the town, marched by Fort Pitt in a show of force and departed without destroying the town.

Left: A statue of whiskey rebels stands in downtown Washington, Pennsylvania. This area was the center of the 1790s Whiskey Rebellion. *Author.*

Below: For two days, the rebels fired on Neville's house, which was defended by the people he enslaved and some soldiers from Fort Pitt. *Author's collection.*

With federal authority threatened, President Washington called out fourteen thousand troops from Pennsylvania, Maryland, New Jersey and Virginia. Leading them in person, he was the only sitting president to actively command troops in the field. The army marched west, and by October 1794, it had taken control in Washington County and Pittsburgh. With troops in their midst, the rebellion collapsed.

Forty rebels were arrested, and twenty were sent to Philadelphia for trial. Two were found guilty of treason but were pardoned by Washington. David Bradford, one of the outspoken leaders of the rebellion, fled to the Louisiana Territory. In November, the army departed, having cost the government over $500,000 to suppress the rebellion.

President Thomas Jefferson repealed the tax law in 1802, noting it was impossible to collect. The rebellion was the first major test for the young national government and also illustrates the east-west rift between the settled area of Pennsylvania and the lawless frontier.

SITES TO VISIT

BOWER HILL SITE
GPS: 40 22.458, -80 5.167

The only battle of the rebellion took place here on a site marked with only a historic marker. The marker is located on Kane Boulevard, one-quarter mile west of Bower Hill Road. There are no facilities at this site.

BRADFORD HOUSE
175 SOUTH MAIN STREET | WASHINGTON, PA 15301
724-222-3604 | WWW.BRADFORDHOUSE.ORG
GPS: 40 16.8182, -80 24.5003

Tour the house of one of the rebellion's leaders, David Bradford. Built in 1786, it is also one of the oldest homes in the city of Washington, Pennsylvania.

CENTURY INN
2175 EAST NATIONAL PIKE | SCENERY HILL, PA 15360
724-945-6600 | WWW.HILLSTAVERN.WORDPRESS.COM
GPS: 40 8.6124, -80 7.0001

Enjoy a sample of whiskey at the place where it happened. This tavern along the National Road dates to 1794 and displays an original Whiskey Rebellion flag in its bar room.

FORT CUMBERLAND SITE

Part of the federal army gathered here. See page 98.

Detail from the marker on Washington's headquarters building in Cumberland. *Author's collection.*

MINGO CREEK PRESBYTERIAN CHURCH CEMETERY
561 MINGO CHURCH ROAD | FINLEYVILLE, PA 15332
WWW.MINGOCHURCH.ORG
GPS: 40 22.9668, -79 99.7170

Here, many important Whiskey Rebels are buried, and their gravestones marked. James McFarlane, killed at Bower Hill, is probably the most famous person who rests here.

OLIVER MILLER HOMESTEAD
1 STONE MANSE DRIVE | SOUTH PARK, PA 15129
412-835-1554
WWW.ALLEGHENYCOUNTY.US/PARKS/SOUTH-PARK/OLIVER-MILLER-HOMESTEAD
GPS: 40 31.9683, -80 0.7874

The stone Oliver Miller house dates to 1772. Oliver's son William resided nearby, and federal agents came to his house to fine him for failing to register his still. William refused to be served the writ, and his neighbors came and fired at the departing officers. The home and gardens are open for tours.

WOODVILLE PLANTATION
1375 WASHINGTON PIKE | BRIDGEVILLE, PA 15017
412-221-0348 | WWW.WOODVILLE-EXPERIENCE.ORG
GPS: 40 37.9845, -80 9.6001

Built in 1775, this was the home of tax collector John Neville. The historic site is open for tours and holds special events.

GEORGE WASHINGTON'S VISITS TO WESTERN PENNSYLVANIA

It is a common claim among the historic sites of the East Coast that "George Washington slept here." He traveled extensively during the eight years of the Revolution and the eight years he served as president. Washington is also strongly associated with Virginia, especially his home region of northern Virginia. Yet outside that part of Virginia, there is only one area he regularly visited throughout his life: western Pennsylvania.

From his first journey into the region as an unknown, inexperienced young militia officer to his last appearance here as a nationally recognized leader, it seems Washington visited the area ten times. Each of these trips into the Laurel Highlands represents a different phase in Washington's life.

1. In 1753, twenty-one-year-old Washington, a major in the Virginia militia, left Williamsburg with a note from Governor Dinwiddie to deliver to the French. Washington traveled with guide Chirstopher Gist and six others, mostly Native traders. As Washington passed through the region in mid-October, the journey was difficult, and he wrote of "excessive rains and vast quantities of snow."

2. Washington returned in early January 1754 on the same path, perhaps making note of familiar landmarks. He was lucky to be alive, having survived a fall into the icy Allegheny River and an assassination attempt by a hostile Native.

A quiet stretch of the Braddock/Nemacolin Road encourages one to reflect on the many people—famous and little known—who have traveled this road over its hundreds of years. *Author's collection.*

Fort Necessity's site in the mid-twentieth century, showing how open the ground was. *New York Public Library.*

3. At the head of a detachment of Virginia militia, Washington arrived in mid-May 1754. He eventually attacked French troops at Jumonville Glen (his first battle) and then retreated to Fort Necessity. There, he surrendered (the only time he ever would) on July 4.

4. Washington and his Virginia troops retreated along the road, returning over the mountains to report to the governor on what had transpired. While riding along, Washington had time to reflect on the heart-pounding days of late June and early July and his first two battles—one victory, one defeat— where he saw men killed in combat and heard the whistle of the musket balls (which he found "charming"). Did he second guess his decisions as he rode over the mountains?

5. Accompanying General Braddock's army, Washington trod the old road again in June 1755. He was very ill but made the journey, anxious to be with the army when they met the French. On this passage of the road, Washington was jostled along in a wagon, as he was too weak to ride from his "violent" illness.

6. Braddock's forces met defeat on July 9 along the Monongahela River. Washington survived with bullet holes in his coat and hat. He helped oversee the withdrawal of the army and again returned to Virginia over the old path in mid-July.

In the years ahead, Washington was married, participated in the successful Forbes campaign (capturing Fort Duquesne and ousting the French for good), was elected to public office and inherited Mount Vernon.

7. On October 12, 1770, Washington arrived to inspect his western lands. He wrote that day that he rode twenty miles, "which we found a tolerable good day's work. The country we travelled over today was very mountainous

and stony, with but very little good land." It had been fifteen years since he passed by the fern-covered hills and rocky outcroppings along the road.

By 1770, tensions with the mother country would have dominated Washington's thoughts. The Boston Massacre took place that March. As a landowner and member of Virginia's House of Burgesses, Washington was no doubt concerned about the future.

8. He returned from inspecting his lands in 1770, having journeyed all the way to the small town of Pittsburgh at the Forks of the Ohio River. Washington was entitled to land grants from Virginia for his service in the French and Indian War. This area of modern western Pennsylvania was claimed by both Virginia and Pennsylvania, and the border would not be settled until the Revolution was nearly over.

9. In 1784, with the Revolution over for just one year, Washington again traveled the old road to the west. He had been away from his beloved Mount Vernon for eight years with only one brief visit, but after the war, it did not take long for him to turn to his valuable lands. He not only visited his holdings, but he also added to them, purchasing the Great Meadows, where the Battle of Fort Necessity took place thirty years earlier.

How many people can say they bought their own battlefield? Having commanded large armies and seen much in his military career, Washington no doubt looked over the ruins of the fort and the shallow trenches around it with reflection. July 4 had a different meaning for him now.

It wasn't all about nostalgia, as there was serious business at hand as well. Washington had many squatters on his land who refused to leave or recognize his claims. The former commander in chief settled with these unruly frontiersmen, agreeing to let them stay in exchange for payments (which he deemed below value). Although he was revered across the nation, in this remote corner, frontier families who squatted on the war hero's land and refused to negotiate with him.

10. Washington returned east, heading toward home and retirement—and eventually the presidency. This was Washington's last journey over this section of the road. In the decades ahead, it would see the march of an army to suppress the Whiskey Rebellion and floods of settlers and travelers on the National Road.

WASHINGTON VISITED THE AREA during the different stages of his life: as a young militia officer, as a seasoned combat veteran, as a husband and homeowner, as an aspiring politician and as a war hero.

Today, there is a Washington County in southwestern Pennsylvania, with the city of Washington as its seat. He is also remembered with Washington and Jefferson University; several elementary, middle and high schools in the region; and a bridge in Pittsburgh.

NOTES

Chapter 1

1. Downes, *Council Fires*, ix, 18.
2. Ward, *Breaking the Backcountry*, 88; Wallace, *Indians in Pennsylvania*, 3; Jennings, *Empire of Fortune*, 265; Anderson, *Crucible*, 18; Downes, *Council Fires*, 20. After 1722, the Tuscarora joined the confederacy from their home in the Carolinas, and the Iroquois were known as the Six Nations.
3. Ward, *Breaking the Backcountry*, 59–60.
4. Downes, *Council Fires*, 38.
5. Wallace, *Indians in Pennsylvania*, 173; Swift, *Mid-Appalachian Frontier*, 9.
6. Wallace, *Indians in Pennsylvania*, 126; Downes, *Council Fires*, 19.
7. Wallace, *Indians in Pennsylvania*, 29, 139; Downes, *Council Fires*, 43.
8. Wallace, *Indians in Pennsylvania*, 60, 140.
9. Crytzer, *Washington's Pittsburgh*, 40; Wallace, *Indians in Pennsylvania*, 128.
10. Wenning, *Fort Duquesne and Fort Pitt*, 142.
11. Misencik, *Washington and the Half-King*, 84.
12. Jennings, *Empire of Fortune*, 260.
13. Ibid., 8, 52.
14. Jacobs, *Wilderness Politics*, 87.
15. Parkman, *Montcalm and Wolfe*, 1,070; Anderson, *Crucible*, 184; Jennings, *Empire of Fortune*, 207; Downes, *Council Fires*, 20, 76–78.
16. Jennings, *Empire of Fortune*, 29.
17. Downes, *Council Fires*, 29; Jennings, *Empire of Fortune*, 33, 96.
18. Jennings, *Empire of Fortune*, 52–53.
19. Ibid., 50, 54.

Chapter 2

1. Crytzer, *Washington's Pittsburgh*, 33.
2. Ibid., 29; Kent, *French Invasion*, 15; Powell, *Fort Cumberland*, 2; Lambing, *Register of Fort Duquesne*, 2.
3. Lambing, *Register of Fort Duquesne*, 3, 2.
4. Kent, *French Invasion*, 7, 9.
5. Jennings, *Empire of Fortune*, 16.
6. Kent, *French Invasion*, 11; Trudel, *Jumonville Affair*, 5.
7. Schoenfield, *Fort De La Presqu'ile*, 17, 20–21.
8. Ibid., 18.
9. Kent, *French Invasion*, 27.
10. Schoenfield, *Fort De La Presqu'ile*, 38–9; Kent, *French Invasion*, 31.
11. Ward, *Breaking the Backcountry*, 11; Schoenfield, *Fort De La Presqu'ile*, 40.
12. Schoenfield, *Fort De La Presqu'ile*, 40; Gallup, *Memoir*, 54.
13. Kent, *French Invasion*, 31.
14. Schoenfield, *Fort De La Presqu'ile*, 17; Kent, *French Invasion*, 33.
15. Stotz, *Outposts of the War*, 75.
16. Kent, *French Invasion*, 34.
17. Ibid., 56, 64.
18. Lambing, *Register of Fort Duquesne*, 23.
19. Kent, *French Invasion*, 60, 64.
20. Ibid., 58–59.
21. Downes, *Council Fires*, 63.
22. Kent, *French Invasion*, 45–50.
23. Trudel, *Jumonville Affair*, 7–8.
24. Kent, *French Invasion*, 64; Misencik, *Washington and the Half-King*, 85.

Chapter 3

1. Powell, *Fort Cumberland*, 1.
2. Crytzer, *Washington's Pittsburgh*, 36–7; Axelrod, *Bloodletting*, 83.
3. Powell, *Fort Cumberland*, 9.
4. Ibid., 9–16.
5. Ibid., 20, 24.
6. Misencik, *Washington and the Half-King*, 62; *Journal of Major George Washington*, 3.
7. Kent, *Washington's Journal*, 4.
8. Crytzer, *Washington's Pittsburgh*, 40; Kent, *Washington's Journal*, 5.
9. Misencik, *Washington and the Half-King*, 66–67.
10. Jennings, *Empire of Fortune*, 60–61.
11. Crytzer, *Washington's Pittsburgh*, 50–64; Kent, *Washington's Journal*, 6–7.
12. Axelrod, *Bloodletting*, 96–99.
13. Ibid., 99, 101; Jennings, *Empire of Fortune*, 62.
14. Axelrod, *Bloodletting*, 105, 174.

15. Kent, *Washington's Journal*, 13.
16. Ibid.
17. Crytzer, *Washington's Pittsburgh*, 80; Kent, *Washington's Journal*, 15.
18. Crytzer, *Washington's Pittsburgh*, 89–90; Kent, *Washington's Journal*, 16.
19. Crytzer, *Washington's Pittsburgh*, 91; Kent, *Washington's Journal*, 16; Axelrod, *Bloodletting*, 117–18.
20. *Journal of Major George Washington*, 17.
21. Crytzer, *Washington's Pittsburgh*, 93, 96; Kent, *Washington's Journal*, 19.
22. Axelrod, *Bloodletting*, 119, 122; Crytzer, *Washington's Pittsburgh*, 93, 98.
23. Kent, *Washington's Journal*, 20.
24. Crytzer, *Washington's Pittsburgh*, 105–6; Kent, *Washington's Journal*, 20–21.
25. Crytzer, *Washington's Pittsburgh*, 107.
26. Kent, *Washington's Journal*, 21.
27. Crytzer, *Washington's Pittsburgh*, 114–15.
28. Ibid., 111; Kent, *Washington's Journal*, 27–28.
29. Zagarri, *Life of General Washington*, xxvi.
30. Misencik, *Washington and the Half-King*, 82; Cherry, *Pittsburgh's Lost Outpost*, 25, 28.
31. Misencik, *Washington and the Half-King*, 90; Ward, *Breaking the Backcountry*, 33.
32. Misencik, *Washington and the Half-King*, 86–88, 90–91.
33. Schoenfield, *Fort De La Presqu'ile*, 24; Misencik, *Washington and the Half-King*, 85; Downes, *Council Fires*, 64.
34. Misencik, *Washington and the Half-King*, 94–96.
35. Ibid., 97.
36. Lambing, *Register of Fort Duquesne*, 27.
37. Misencik, *Washington and the Half-King*, 98–100.
38. Schoenfield, *Fort De La Presqu'ile*, 2–3.

Chapter 4

1. Gallup, *Memoir*, xv, 2, 24, 48–49.
2. Ibid., 93.
3. Lambing, *Register of Fort Duquesne*, 57, 65, 69; Trudel, *Jumonville Affair*, 10; Peyser, *Ambush and Revenge*, 1. The register from Fort Duquesne indicates that children were born and baptized at the fort, though the number of French women who lived there is not known. Dumas and Contrecoeur, in addition to being the fort's commanders, were also godfathers to several children.
4. Trudel, *Jumonville Affair*, 11.
5. Kent, *Washington's Journal*, 9.
6. Ibid., 13–14.
7. Misencik, *Washington and the Half-King*, 104; Kent, *Washington's Journal*, 33; Abbot, *Papers of George Washington*, 1:100.
8. Misencik, *Washington and the Half-King*, 105–6.
9. Downes, *Council Fires*, 73.

10. Misencik, *Washington and the Half-King*, 107; Kent, *Washington's Journal*, 15.
11. Misencik, *Washington and the Half-King*, 108; Kent, *Washington's Journal*, 18; Abbot, *Papers of George Washington*, 1:113.
12. Misencik, *Washington and the Half-King*, 108–9.
13. Abbot, *Papers of George Washington*, 1:131.
14. Misencik, *Washington and the Half-King*, 111; Abbot, *Papers of George Washington*, 1:110.
15. Preston, *Braddock's Defeat*, 27, 351–53.
16. Misencik, *Washington and the Half-King*, 111–14, 123; Kent, *Washington's Journal*, 16.
17. Kent, *Washington's Journal*, 17–18.
18. Misencik, *Washington and the Half-King*, 114–15.
19. Trudel, *Jumonville Affair*, 16.
20. Ibid., 17–18.
21. Ibid., 20–21.
22. Ibid., 22.
23. Misencik, *Washington and the Half-King*, 116–17.
24. Trudel, *Jumonville Affair*, 12.
25. Ibid., 13.
26. Misencik, *Washington and the Half-King*, 122.
27. Ibid., 122–23; Kent, *Washington's Journal*, 18.
28. Misencik, *Washington and the Half-King*, 123; Kent, *Washington's Journal*, 19; Abbot, *Papers of George Washington*, 1:124.
29. Misencik, *Washington and the Half-King*, 128–30; Axelrod, *Bloodletting*, 202; Abbot, *Papers of George Washington*, 1:129.
30. Axelrod, *Bloodletting*, 212; Misencik, *Washington and the Half-King*, 134.
31. Harrington, *New Light*, 67; Axelrod, *Bloodletting*, 214.
32. Misencik, *Washington and the Half-King*, 106; Abbot, *Papers of George Washington*, 1:105; Axelrod, *Bloodletting*, 201.
33. Ward, *Breaking the Backcountry*, 34.
34. Harrington, *New Light*, 68.
35. Ward, *Breaking the Backcountry*, 34; Peyser, *Ambush and Revenge*, 21.
36. Peyser, *Ambush and Revenge*, 5; Gallup, *Memoir*, 104; Harrington, *New Light*, 64.
37. Harrington, *New Light*, 64.
38. Gallup, *Memoir*, 100–1.
39. Misencik, *Washington and the Half-King*, 139; Harrington, *New Light*, 65; Abbot, *Papers of George Washington*, 1:159–60.
40. Axelrod, *Bloodletting*, 226–27.
41. Harrington, *New Light*, 68; Misencik, *Washington and the Half-King*, 142.
42. Harrington, *New Light*, 64–65.
43. Misencik, *Washington and the Half-King*, 143; Axelrod, *Bloodletting*, 230.
44. Misencik, *Washington and the Half-King*, 144–45; Axelrod, *Bloodletting*, 240.
45. Misencik, *Washington and the Half-King*, 146–47; Axelrod, *Bloodletting*, 232, 238–39.
46. Axelrod, *Bloodletting*, 249; Gallup, *Memoir*, 104.

47. Misencik, *Washington and the Half-King*, 148.
48. Ibid., 149; Axelrod, *Bloodletting*, 236.
49. Misencik, *Washington and the Half-King*, 150.
50. Harrington, *New Light*, 64.
51. Ibid.
52. Ibid., 65.
53. Ibid., 65–66.
54. Misencik, *Washington and the Half-King*, 151, 171; Downes, *Council Fires*, 73.
55. Kent, *Washington's Journal*, 2; Axelrod, *Bloodletting*, 242–43.
56. Kent, *Washington's Journal*, 2.
57. Ibid., 2–6.
58. Ibid., 6–7.
59. Peyser, *Ambush and Revenge*, 26.
60. *Fort Necessity and Historic Shrines*, 11–16; Harrington, *New Light*, 19.
61. *Fort Necessity and Historic Shrines*, 18, 63; Harrington, *New Light*, 19.
62. Harrington, *New Light*, 8.
63. Ibid., 19–20.
64. Ibid., 9, 20.
65. Powell, *Fort Cumberland*, 11.
66. Ibid., 11–13.

Chapter 5

1. Ward, *Breaking the Backcountry*, 71.
2. Messner, *Reflections*, 14–15, 54–55.
3. Crocker, *Braddock's March*, 52, 49.
4. Harris, *Orderly Books*, 20.
5. Harris, *Orderly Books*, 73–74; Abbot, *Papers of George Washington*, 1:299.
6. Dunkerly, *Women of the Revolution*, 9–10, 14–19; Harris, *Orderly Books*, 80.
7. Crocker, *Braddock's March*, 96; Preston, *Braddock's Defeat*, 79–82.
8. Harris, *Orderly Books*, 20.
9. Crocker, *Braddock's March*, 116–18; Abbot, *Papers of George Washington*, 1:301.
10. Harris, *Orderly Books*, 21.
11. Preston, *Braddock's Defeat*, 110–21. Historian David Preston takes a careful look at this crucial aspect of the campaign.
12. Powell, *Fort Cumberland*, 21; Harris, *Orderly Books*, 21; Lacock, *Braddock Road*, 6–7.
13. Crocker, *Braddock's March*, 260–70; Preston, *Braddock's Defeat*, 109.
14. Crocker, *Braddock's March*, 284–85.
15. Harris, *Orderly Books*, 180; Abbot, *Papers of George Washington*, 1:321.
16. Harris, *Orderly Books*, 181; Wahll, *Braddock Road Chronicles*, 310; Messner, *Reflections*, 22–24.
17. Crocker, *Braddock's March*, 183.
18. Harris, *Orderly Books*, 307; Wahll, *Braddock Road Chronicles*, 296–97.

NOTES TO PAGES 84–92

20. Wahll, *Braddock Road Chronicles*, 303, 305.
21. Preston, *Braddock's Defeat*, 201.
22. Harris, *Orderly Books*, 22, 70; Abbot, *Papers of George Washington*, 1:319.
23. Crocker, *Braddock's March*, 194; Preston, *Braddock's Defeat*, 199, 201, 211.
24. Crocker, *Braddock's March*, 194.
25. Wahll, *Braddock Road Chronicles*, 330; Preston, *Braddock's Defeat*, 204.
26. Preston, *Braddock's Defeat*, 204–5.
27. Ibid., 206–7; Crocker, *Braddock's March*, 194.
28. Preston, *Braddock's Defeat*, 217.
29. Crocker, *Braddock's March*, 209.
30. Preston, *Braddock's Defeat*, 208–9; Lambing, *Register of Fort Duquesne*, 37, 63; Gallup, *Memoir*, 130–31.
31. Messner, *Reflections*, 43; Preston, *Braddock's Defeat*, 157, 337. Tradition places the famous Native Charles Langlade here, but there is no evidence of it. His name does not appear on any of the French officer rolls (Langlade was an ensign in 1755). Both Michael McDonnell and Charles Trap—authors of biographies of Langlade—also conclude he was not present.
32. Crocker, *Braddock's March*, 206.
33. Lambing, *Register of Fort Duquesne*, 37 63; Gallup, *Memoir*, 130–31.
34. Gallup, *Memoir*, 131.
35. Scott, *Colorful Characters*, 3, 5–7.
36. Preston, *Braddock's Defeat*, 356.
37. Crocker, *Braddock's March*, 214.
38. Messner, *Reflections*, 48.
39. Gallup, *Memoir*, 130.
40. Ibid., 141.
41. Preston, *Braddock's Defeat*, 234.
42. Crocker, *Braddock's March*, 214.
43. Harris, *Orderly Books*, 193–95; Abbot, *Papers of George Washington*, 1:339.
44. Crocker, *Braddock's March*, 212.
45. Ibid., 215; Preston, *Braddock's Defeat*, 238.
46. Preston, *Braddock's Defeat*, 235.
47. Crocker, *Braddock's March*, 219; Preston, *Braddock's Defeat*, 252.
48. Crocker, *Braddock's March*, 220; Preston, *Braddock's Defeat*, 263.
49. Preston, *Braddock's Defeat*, 232–33.
50. Gallup, *Memoir*, 131; Wenning, *Fort Duquesne and Fort Pitt*, 57.
51. Preston, *Braddock's Defeat*, 265.
52. Lambing, *Register of Fort Duquesne*, 4–5, 37.
53. Preston, *Braddock's Defeat*, 273.
54. Ibid., 319; O'Meara, *Guns at the Forks*, 155; Brown, "Journal of Charlotte Brown," 176, 182–83.
55. Preston, *Braddock's Defeat*, 319; Miller, *Early Land Marks*, 15.

56. Dunkerly, "Battlefield Guide."
57. Messner, *Reflections*, 54–55.

Chapter 6

1. Downes, *Council Fires*, 75; Ward, *Breaking the Backcountry*, 65.
2. Seymour, *Pennsylvania Associators*, 71.
3. Ward, *Breaking the Backcountry*, 57.
4. Ibid., 126–28.
5. Seymour, *Pennsylvania Associators*, 43–44.
6. Ward, *Breaking the Backcountry*, 125, 97; Seymour, *Pennsylvania Associators*, 71–72.
7. Ward, *Breaking the Backcountry*, 97.
8. Seymour, *Pennsylvania Associators*, 77–78.
9. Wenning, *Fort Duquesne and Fort Pitt*, 58.
10. Ibid., 59.
11. Downes, *Council Fires*, 81.
12. Ward, *Breaking the Backcountry*, 101; Powell, *Fort Cumberland*, 26, 39.
13. O'Meara, *Guns at the Forks*, 174.
14. Ibid., 171; Ward, *Breaking the Backcountry*, 148; Schoenfield, *Fort De La Presqu'ile*, 52.
15. Wenning, *Fort Duquesne and Fort Pitt*, 15.
16. Jennings, *Empire of Fortune*, 355; Ward, *Breaking the Backcountry*, 98, 159.
17. Crytzer, *Washington's Pittsburgh*, 19.
18. Messner, *Reflections*, 50–51.
19. Ward, *Breaking the Backcountry*, 156.
20. Powell, *Fort Cumberland*, 26–39; O'Meara, *Guns at the Forks*, 158.
21. Frothingham, *Washington: Commander in Chief*, 22–23; Abbot, *Papers of George Washington*, 2:334.
22. Freeman, *George Washington*, 1:2, 254–59; Abbot, *Papers of George Washington*, 2:88.
23. Ward, *Breaking the Backcountry*, 158.

Chapter 7

1. Cubbison, *British Defeat*, 6.
2. Abbot, *Papers of George Washington*, 5:118, 353, 376.
3. Powell, *Fort Cumberland*, 27.
4. Ibid., 28.
5. Stevens, Kent and Leonard, *Papers of Henry Bouquet*, 2:265.
6. Cubbison, *British Defeat*, 17; McConnell, *To Risk It All*, 56.
7. James and Stotz, *Drums in the Forest*, 44–4; McConnell, *To Risk It All*, 76. The Cherokee and Catawaba, although far removed from the events in the Ohio Country and New York frontier, were being drawn into the conflict as it escalated. French and British agents vied for their support as the war expanded into the Southeast.
8. Stevens, Kent and Leonard, *Papers of Henry Bouquet*, 2:134–35, 439, 477.

NOTES TO PAGES 122-130

9. Ibid., 111.
10. James and Stotz, *Drums in the Forest*, 45; Abbot, *Papers of George Washington*, 5:213–14. Washington noted that the escaped enslaved man was "well acquainted with the Ohio." Later known as Frank, he reached Williamsburg and attained his freedom.
11. James and Stotz, *Drums in the Forest*, 46.
12. Ibid., 47. Forbes visited sites later occupied by the Confederate army in 1863. Although General Braddock had been in Sharpsburg, Maryland, the future site of the battle of Antietam, Forbes was close but did not pass through Gettysburg.
13. Stevens, Kent and Leonard, *Papers of Henry Bouquet*, 2:243.
14. Ibid., 234.
15. Cubbison, *British Defeat*, 99.
16. Ibid.
17. Ibid., 100; Stevens, Kent and Leonard, *Papers of Henry Bouquet*, 2:414.
18. James and Stotz, *Drums in the Forest*, 49; West, *Fort Ligonier*, 6; Stotz, *Fort Ligonier*, 1, 3.
19. Stotz, *Fort Ligonier*, 3; Cubbison, *British Defeat*, 123.
20. McCulloch and Todish, *Through So Many Dangers*, 38.
21. Cubbison, *British Defeat*, 124–25.
22. Ibid., 130-2; Abbot, *Papers of George Washington*, 6:38–39.
23. McCulloch and Todish, *Through So Many Dangers*, 40–41; Stevens, Kent and Leonard, *Papers of Henry Bouquet*, 2:533, 539.
24. West, *Fort Ligonier*, 7; James and Stotz, *Drums in the Forest*, 50.
25. West, *Fort Ligonier*, 7; James and Stotz, *Drums in the Forest*, 50; Cubbison, *British Defeat*, 151–52; Abbot, *Papers of George Washington*, 6:121–22.
26. West, *Fort Ligonier*, 7; James and Stotz, *Drums in the Forest*, 51; Abbot, *Papers of George Washington*, 6:119.
27. James and Stotz, *Drums in the Forest*, 52.
28. West, *Fort Ligonier*, 12.
29. Grimm, *Archaeological Investigation*, 5, 7–8, 175, 184.
30. Downes, *Council Fires*, 82; McConnell, *To Risk It All*, 82–83, 135.
31. Downes, *Council Fires*, 84.
32. Ibid., 86–87, 91.
33. Ibid., 89.
34. Ibid., 88.
35. Stevens, Kent and Leonard, *Papers of Henry Bouquet*, 2:162–63, 168; Abbot, *Papers of George Washington*, 6:129.
36. Cherry, *Pittsburgh's Lost Outpost*, 97.
37. Stevens, Kent and Leonard, *Papers of Henry Bouquet*, 2:495, 542; Abbot, *Papers of George Washington*, 6:156.
38. Stotz, *Outposts of the War*, 135; Abbot, *Papers of George Washington*, 6:158.
39. Lambing, *Register of Fort Duquesne*, 30.
40. Schoenfield, *Fort De La Presqu'ile*, 34–37.
41. Cubbison, *British Defeat*, 172.
42. Abbot, *Papers of George Washington*, 6:158.

43. Stevens, Kent and Leonard, *Papers of Henry Bouquet*, 2:614.
44. Barton, letter to the *Pennsylvania Gazette*.
45. Messner, *Reflections*, 10–11; Cubbison, *British Defeat*, 175.
46. Crytzer, *Fort Pitt*, 17–18, 22–23; Cubbison, *British Defeat*, 175.
47. Crytzer, *Fort Pitt*, 20, 25, 24.
48. Ibid., 38, 45–46, 48.
49. Ibid., 49; Dixon, *Museum Guide*, 42.
50. Crytzer, *Fort Pitt*, 51.
51. Downes, *Council Fires*, 92–94.
52. Ibid., 102.
53. Miller, *Early Land Marks*, 5.
54. Swauger and Lang, "Excavations at the Music Bastion," 33, 35, 38, 43.

Chapter 8

1. Ward, *Breaking the Backcountry*, 190.
2. Jennings, *Empire of Fortune*, 421–25.
3. Downes, *Council Fires*, 104–5; Ward, *Breaking the Backcountry*, 210–11.
4. Downes, *Council Fires*, 105–6, 109; Ward, *Breaking the Backcountry*, 186, 202.
5. Dixon, *Never Come to Peace Again*, 41.
6. Downes, *Council Fires*, 113.
7. Ward, *Breaking the Backcountry*, 25, 186.
8. Weaver, *Fort Pitt Blockhouse*, 21.
9. Ward, *Breaking the Backcountry*, 202.
10. Downes, *Council Fires*, 114.
11. Ibid., 117–18.
12. Ibid., 119.
13. Weaver, *Fort Pitt Blockhouse*, 21.
14. Crytzer, *Fort Pitt*, 108, 109; Dixon, *Never Come to Peace Again*, 30–31.
15. Weaver, *Fort Pitt Blockhouse*, 21; Cherry, *Pittsburgh's Lost Outpost*, 97; Waddell, *Papers of Henry Bouquet*, 6:202.
16. Dixon, *Never Come to Peace Again*, 31, 32.
17. Weaver, *Fort Pitt Blockhouse*, 25, 28–30.
18. Dixon, *Never Come to Peace Again*, 32.
19. Ibid., 31.
20. Ibid., 32.
21. McCulloch and Todish, *Through So Many Dangers*, 88–90.
22. Ibid., 90; Daudelin, "Numbers and Tactics," 153.
23. Weaver, *Fort Pitt Blockhouse*, 23; McCulloch and Todish, *Through So Many Dangers*, 90; Daudelin, "Numbers and Tactics," 153.
24. Crytzer, *Fort Pitt*, 116.
25. Ibid., 117; McCulloch and Todish, *Through So Many Dangers*, 92.
26. Dixon, *Never Come to Peace Again*, 190; Wallace, *Indians in Pennsylvania*, 175.

27. Daudelin, "Numbers and Tactics," 164–65.
28. McCulloch and Todish, *Through So Many Dangers*, 94.
29. Crytzer, *Fort Pitt*, 120; Dixon, *Museum Guide*, 32.
30. Smith, *Account of Bouquet's Expedition*, 34.
31. Ibid., 35.
32. McCulloch and Todish, *Through So Many Dangers*, 42.
33. Smith, *Account of Bouquet's Expedition*, 65.
34. Weaver, *Fort Pitt Blockhouse*, 33; Dixon, *Bushy Run*, 34.
35. Dixon, *Bushy Run*, 36–37.
36. Weaver, *Fort Pitt Blockhouse*, 38.
37. Dixon, *Bushy Run*, 41; Weaver, *Fort Pitt Blockhouse*, 65, 132.
38. Dixon, *Bushy Run*, 39.
39. Ibid., 16.
40. Ibid., 12.

Chapter 9

1. Ward, *Breaking the Backcountry*, 256.
2. Dowd, *War Under Heaven*, 205.
3. Ward, *Breaking the Backcountry*, 3–4, 256.

Appendix A

1. Fitzpatrick, *Writings of Washington*, 3:292–93.
2. Ibid., 6:346.
3. Freeman, *George Washington*, 1:284, 329.
4. Ibid., 330, 342, 381.
5. Ibid., 327, 407.
6. Flexner, *Indispensable Man*, 18, 23.
7. O'Meara, *Guns at the Forks*, 127, 132.
8. Ibid., 138.
9. Frothingham, *Washington: Commander in Chief*, 22–23.
10. Freeman, *George Washington*, 1:2, 254–59.
11. Flexner, *Indispensable Man*, 33–34; Jennings, *Empire of Fortune*, 406.
12. Flexner, *Indispensable Man*, 34; Freeman, *George Washington*, 1:2, 360.
13. Frothingham, *Washington: Commander in Chief*, 29.
14. Fitzpatrick, *Writings of Washington*, 6:5.
15. Ibid., 4:202.

BIBLIOGRAPHY

Abbot, W.W., ed. *The Papers of George Washington*. Vol. 1. Charlottesville: University of Virginia Press, 1983.

———. *The Papers of George Washington*. Vol. 2. Charlottesville: University of Virginia Press, 1983.

———. *The Papers of George Washington*. Vol. 5. Charlottesville: University of Virginia Press, 1988.

———. *The Papers of George Washington*. Vol. 6. Charlottesville: University of Virginia Press, 1988.

Anderson, Fred. *Crucible of War*. New York: M. Knopf, 2000.

Axelrod, Alan. *Bloodletting at Great Meadows*. Philadelphia, PA: Running Press, 2007.

Barton, Thomas. Letter to the *Pennsylvania Gazette*. November 28, 1758.

Brown, Charlotte. "The Journal of Charlotte Brown, Matron of the General Hospital, with the English Forces in America, 1754–1756." In *Colonial Captivities, Marches and Journeys*. Port Washington, NY: Kennikat Press, 1935.

Cherry, Jason A. *Pittsburgh's Lost Outpost*. Charleston, SC: The History Press, 2019.

Crocker, Thomas E. *Braddock's March*. Yardley, PA: Westholme, 2009.

Crytzer, Brady. *Fort Pitt*. Charleston, SC: The History Press, 2012.

———. *Major Washington's Pittsburgh*. Charleston, SC: The History Press, 2011.

Cubbison, Douglas R. *The British Defeat of the French in Pennsylvania, 1758*. Jefferson, NC: McFarland, 2010.

Daudelin, Don. "Numbers and Tactics at Bushy Run." *Western Pennsylvania Historical Magazine* 68, no. 2 (1985): 153–79.

Dixon, David. *Bushy Run Battlefield*. Mechanicsburg, PA: Stackpole Books, 2003.

———. *Fort Pitt Museum Guide*. Mechanicsburg, PA: Stackpole Books, 2004.

———. *Never Come to Peace Again*. Norman: University of Oklahoma Press, 2005.

Dowd, Gregory. *War Under Heaven*. Baltimore, MD: Johns Hopkins University Press, 2004.

Downes, Randolph C. *Council Fires on the Upper Ohio*. Pittsburgh, PA: University of Pittsburgh Press, 1940.

Dunkerly, Robert M. "A Battlefield Guide to the Battle of Braddock." Unpublished report, 1991.

———. *Women of the Revolution*. Charleston, SC: The History Press, 2007.

Fitzpatrick, John C., ed., *Writings of Washington*. Washington, D.C.: Government Printing Office, 1932.

Flexner, Felix. *Indispensable Man*. Boston: Little, Brown and Company, 1974.

Fort Necessity and Historic Shrines of the Redstone Country. Uniontown: Fort Necessity Chapter, Pennsylvania Society of the Sons of the American Revolution, 1932.

Freeman, Douglass S. *George Washington*. Vol. 1. New York: Charles Scribner's Sons, 1948.

Frothingham, Thomas. *George Washington: Commander in Chief*. Boston, MA: Houghton-Mifflin Co., 1930.

Gallup, Andrew, ed. *Memoir of a French and Indian War Soldier*. Westminster, MD: Heritage Books, 1993.

Grimm, Jacob L. *Archaeological Investigation of Fort Ligonier*. Vol. 42. Pittsburgh, PA: Annals of Carnegie Museum, 1970.

Harrington, J.C. *New Light on Washington's Fort Necessity*. Richmond, VA: Eastern National, 1970.

Harris, James A., ed. *The Orderly Books of Major General Edward Braddock*. Normal, IL: Normal Warfare Publications, 2005.

Hunter, William A. *Forts on the Pennsylvania Frontier*. Lewisburg, PA: Wennawoods Publishing, 1999.

Jacobs, Wilbur. *Wilderness Politics and Indian Affairs*. Lincoln: University of Nebraska Press, 1950.

James, Alfred Proctor, and Charles Morse Stotz. *Drums in the Forest*. Pittsburgh, PA: University of Pittsburgh Press, 2005.

Jennings, Francis. *Empire of Fortune*. New York: WW Norton and Co., 1988.

The Journal of Major George Washington. Williamsburg, VA: Colonial Williamsburg Foundation, 1959.

Kent, Donald, ed. *Contrecoeur's Copy of George Washington's Journal for 1754*. Fort Washington, PA: Eastern National, 1989.

Kent, Donald. *The French Invasion of Western Pennsylvania*. Harrisburg: Pennsylvania Historical and Museum Commission, 1981.

Kummerow, Burton K., Christine H. O'Toole and R. Scott Stephenson. *Pennsylvania's Forbes Trail*. Lanham, MD: Taylor Trade Publishing, 2008.

Lacock, John Kennedy. *Braddock Road*. N.p., 1909.

Lamb, George H. *The Unwritten History of Braddock's Field*. Westminster, MD: Heritage Books, 1907.

Lambing, A.A. *Register of Fort Duquesne*. Pittsburgh, PA: St. Joseph's Protectory Print, 1954.

McConnell, Michael N. *To Risk It All*. Pittsburgh, PA: University of Pittsburgh Press, 2020.

McCulloch, Ian, and Timothy Todish, eds. *Through So Many Dangers: The Memoirs and Adventures of Robert Kirk, Late of the Royal Highland Regiment.* Fleischmanns, NY: Purple Mountain Press, 2004.

Messner, Robert T. *Reflections from Braddock's Battlefield.* North Braddock, PA: Braddock's Field Historical Society, 2005.

Miller, Annie Clark. *Early Land Marks and Old Names in Pittsburgh.* Pittsburgh, PA: Daughters of the American Revolution, 1924.

Misencik, Paul R. *George Washington and the Half-King Tanacharison.* Jefferson, NC: McFarland and Co., 2014.

O'Meara, Walter. *Guns at the Forks.* Englewood Cliffs, NJ: Prentice Hall, 1965.

Parkman, Francis. *Montcalm and Wolfe.* New York: Literary Classics of the United States, 1983.

Peyser, Joseph L. *Ambush and Revenge.* Dunbar, PA: Stefano's Printing, 1999.

Powell, Allan. *Christopher Gist, Frontier Scout.* Shippensburg, PA: Burd Street Press, 1992.

————. *Fort Cumberland.* Parsons, WV: McClain Printing, 1989.

Preston, David L. *Braddock's Defeat.* New York: Oxford University Press, 2015.

Schoenfield, Max. *Fort De La Presqu'ile.* Erie, PA: Erie County Historical Society, 1989.

Scott, Brandon. *Colorful Characters.* Valparariso, IN: Eagle Talon Traders, 2005.

Seymour, Joseph. *Pennsylvania Associators.* Yardley, PA: Westholme, 2012.

Smith, William. *Historical Account of Bouquet's Expedition Against the Ohio Indians in 1764.* Lewisburg, PA: Wenawoods Publishing, 2009.

Stevens, S.K., Donald H. Kent and Autumn L. Leonard, eds. *The Papers of Henry Bouquet.* Vol. 2. Harrisburg: Pennsylvania Historical and Museum Commission, 1951.

Stotz, Charles M. *Fort Ligonier.* Ligonier, PA: Fort Ligonier Memorial Association, 1976.

————. *Outposts of the War for Empire.* Pittsburgh, PA: University of Pittsburgh Press, 1975.

Swauger, James, and Richard Lang. "Excavations at the Music Bastion of Fort Pitt 1964–1965." *Annals of Carnegie Museum* 39, no. 2 (1967): N.p.

Swift, Robert B. *The Mid-Appalachian Frontier.* Gettysburg, PA: Thomas Publications, 2001.

Trudel, Marcel. *The Jumonville Affair.* Fort Washington, PA: Eastern National, 1989.

Waddell, Louis M., ed. *The Papers of Henry Bouquet.* Vol. 6. Harrisburg: Pennsylvania Historical and Museum Commission, 1994.

Wahll, Andrew J. *Braddock Road Chronicles.* Bowie, MD: Heritage Books, 1999.

Wallace, Paul. *Indians in Pennsylvania.* Harrisburg: Pennsylvania Historical and Museum Commission, 1989.

Ward, Matthew C. *Breaking the Backcountry.* Pittsburgh, PA: University of Pittsburgh Press, 2003.

Weaver, Emily M. *The Fort Pitt Blockhouse.* Charleston, SC: The History Press, 2013.

Wenning, Ronald R., ed. *Fort Duquesne and Fort Pitt: The Roots of the French & Indian War.* Lewisburg, PA: Wennawoods Publishing, 2013.

West, Martin. *Fort Ligonier.* Pittsburgh, PA: Knepper Press, 2009.

Zagarri, Rosemarie, ed. *Life of General Washington, by David Humphreys.* Athens: University of Georgia Press, 2006.

INDEX

ABOUT THE AUTHOR

Robert "Bert" M. Dunkerly grew up traveling portions of the Braddock and Forbes Road. One of the first historic sites he visited as a child was Fort Necessity. In the process of researching for this book, he walked, biked and drove the entire lengths of the Braddock and Forbes Roads. He holds a degree in History from St. Vincent College and a masters in historic preservation from Middle Tennessee State University. He has worked at fourteen historic sites and written over a dozen books. He is a past president of the Richmond Civil War Round Table and serves on the Preservation Commission for the American Revolution Round Table–Richmond. Dunkerly is currently a Park Ranger at Richmond National Battlefield Park. He has visited over five hundred battlefields and over one thousand historic sites worldwide. He enjoys exploring local bookstores, battlefields and breweries—not necessarily in that order.